Cover by Magdalena Łozińska

A FEW WORDS FROM THE AUTHOR

It does not matter if you are just preparing to welcome rats in your family, or are among veteran rat owners, or just like me, you are obsessed with everything connected to these amazing creatures, I think you might find some useful and surprising information on the pages of this book. Welcome on a board of rats lovers ship, carrying still small, but steadily growing crew of these critters maniacs!

My adventure with rats began in 2008, I was in high school. It was the first of November, when me and my friend decided to skip school. Having nowhere to go, we ended up at her house. She had a rat, big white and black male, with whom I immediately fell in love, and was seized with the desire to have one on my own. The next day, against my parents' will, I went to the closest pet store and bought Jeffrey – my first rat, whose life was not easy in the beginning. With him I was

Jeffrey, my first rat.

3

learning how to be a good rat mom.

Now, in retrospect, I see that I have made many mistakes in the past. Firstly, I bought Jeff from a store. At that time I was not even aware of the fact that animals other than cats and dogs can be adopted from charities, foster homes or even animal shelters. Taking them home often equals rescuing them. Jeffrey lived his first weeks in a small cage, recommended to me in the pet store, that now (yes, I still have it) is used as a pet carrier. He was a single rat and his diet was not really varied. Hopefully, with the aid of this book, your first rats will have an easier life at the beginning of your adventure.

After some time, when my parents' anger level dropped, they helped me financially, and I was able to buy a bigger cage and better food for Jeff, but I could not get him any company. My parents forbid me from bringing another animal into the house, especially without informing them first. And so there was only me and Jeff for the most of his life.

Later, my sister bought herself a rat. He was aggressive, shy and not very social. She was studying in a different city during this time, and soon found out that she has no time for a pet. So I took him in. His name was Bourbon and he became one of the biggest cuddly fondling I have ever had.

Later came others, Fuga, Dżuma, Kiwi, Chrupka, in pairs or bigger groups, as I learnt how bad it is to keep a single rat. Till this day I had dozens of rats under my care. All of them gave me plenty of beautiful memories, experience and knowledge which I would like to share with you.

INTRODUCTION

What comes to your mind when you hear – RAT? Probably something nice as you decided to reach for this book. Unfortunately, for most of the people this word does not bring pleasant connotations. Some even shudder just at the thought of encountering such an animal on the street, let alone in the house. They feel disgust thinking about the naked hairless tail, often wrongly considered slithery. Often this reluctance is based on cultural cliches and stereotypes, images derived from unfavorable literature or folklore prejudice and shady history of rats.

On the other hand, some people adore and admire these creatures, explore the secrets of their intelligence, exalt them as a masterpiece of Mother Nature. They are indeed fascinating and surprising animals, with exquisite survival skills, easily adopting to very harsh environments. They are excellent climbers and swimmers, they can even hold their breath for up to three minutes! They can balance on a thin rope, even after falling from fifteen meters they can land safely. Rats can jump in the air for around thirty-five inches. They are admirably agile and flexible, can fit through very small holes – if a rat's head fits – the whole body will follow. Their teeth can chew through brick, cinder block or even lead. They are like heroes with superpowers in the animal kingdom but, even despite these amazing abilities, they are rarely perceived as such, rather as villains. It is hard to uproot the image of the rat created by the time and relation between these animals and humans, shaped over thousands of years of living side by side.

HISTORY

The history of coexistence of rats and humans is rather turbulent. From all species around the world we are the most geographically diverse and adaptive ones. The problem in the relationship between us, is the fact that only one side can have a profit from living together, and it is not us. People, on the occasion of leading their own life, created an environment into which rats unintentionally entered, and perfectly adopted. Humans mean an easy source of food, warmth, access to materials to build a nest, and relative safety from predators. On the other hand, for us, rats signify destruction and contamination of food supplies, spread of diseases, and chewed-up clothes. But who are we to blame them? Are we not doing exactly the same to other species? Barging into their lives, usurping their source of food, land, home? By seeking comfortable and easy life we disturb the existence of other animals the same way rats disturb ours, for the same reasons. Luckily for us, rats are much smaller than people.

But starting from the very beginning, where did rats exactly come from? First appearance of the Rodentia order, to which mice, rats, squirrels, beavers, guinea pigs, hamsters, and even prairie dogs and porcupines belong, in the fossil record is dated about 50-60 million years ago, in the Pleistocene. During the emergence of new fauna species, this group of animals developed one common feature, distinguishing them from others – a single pair of continuously growing incisors in their muzzle. The oldest fossils of its representatives come from

Laurasia, the northern part of the Pangea supercontinent. Further migration on a massive scale happened only in the Eocene, and was followed by significant diversification. Rodents started to evolve in various environments, coming in many sizes, and growing different body features. Some of them became naked, some covered in hair, smooth or coarse fur, with long or short tails, bigger ears, adapting to different kinds of lifestyles. Beavers' ancestors settled down near rivers and developed webbed feet. Ancient squirrels evolved to adjust to arboreal life, and forebears of rats and mice grew flexible, slim and agile bodies, thus creating a separate subfamily of Murinae, around 14 million years ago. This large group of mammals, comprising more than five hundred species, occupies a wide variety of habitats: coniferous, deciduous and even tropical forests, savannahs, grasslands, swamps, meadows, even deserts or cities and towns. They have been evolving through millions of years and dividing into many different groups - ancestors of mice, hamsters, gerbils and rats. These last one finally split into two main species – black rat (*Rattus rattus*) and brown rat (*Rattus norvegicus*).

A group of rats is called a mischief. One of the definitions of this word means playful misbehavior, which surely reflects their frolicky temper. Females are termed does, while males - bucks. Their babies are often referred to as pups or pinkies, due to the color of their hairless bodies after birth.

Black rats (*Rattus rattus*) probably originated in India, but quickly spread all over the world around two thousand years ago, seizing the opportunity to travel with people on ships across the seas and oceans – that is why they are often called ship rats. Other nicknames – roof rats or house rats, indicate that they perfectly got used to living among people, and inside their estates. Their fur can be black, gray or brown, with a bright belly. They are most active at night and feed mainly on seeds, fruits and grain, though they are omnivorous, and will not mind a piece of meat for a meal. Living in groups of twenty to even sixty individuals, black rats are a big nuisance for farmers. Reaching out a little more than 7.5 inches without a tail, which can double their length, they are smaller than their cousins – brown rats.

Black rat
Rattus rattus

Brown rats can grow up to almost 12 inches long. Though their Latin name – *Rattus norvegicus* - implies that their country of origin is in the North of Europe, they came from

China. The misleading name was a consequence of the belief that the Vikings brought these creatures on their ships during raids. Indeed, conquers, voyages and over sea trade helped them to quickly disperse around the world, traveling the same method as their cousins. Almost the whole population of brown rats live in the cities, under the surface of the biggest metropolis, that is why they are also called sewer rats. They live in big families and are true omnivores, consuming everything their stomach can digest, mostly food scraps thrown out by people.

Brown rat
Rattus norvegicus

The third most widespread species of rat is the Pacific or Polynesian rat (Rattusexulans), not as famous as their cousins. It also originated in Asia and travelled in ships, reaching mostly shores of Polynesia. Their lifestyle and diet

is similar to the ones of brown and black rats, but they mostly nest in trees. Being excellent climbers, they are able to enrich their diet with eggs or even hatchlings of various birds, bark, and leaves.

This shared life between humans and rats started a long, long time ago. During many archeological excavations a great quantity of mice and rats fossils were found near regions inhabited by humans in ancient times, showing that these animals accompanied us through thousands of years, living in our shadow. Wandering groups of primeval men were a great source of food scraps and protection from many predators, worth following for little creatures dangling at the end of a food chain. Later on, the settled lifestyle brought even more advantages for these rodents – fields bearing grain, gardens full of vegetables and fruits, or pantries, giving access to food all year around. Nonetheless, benefiting from living near us, caused our hatred towards these critters to rise. And finally, came the Black Plague and rats became our worst enemy. Their population skyrocketed, they dominated urban and rural areas. Connecting the dots, people blamed them for the outbreak.

The Bubonic plague indeed stigmatized rats and was a great excuse for us to blame them for the death of tens of millions of people. In the Late Middle Ages the pandemic wiped out one third of the European population, and took a toll also on other continents. Rats, living alongside people and having an easy access to their homes and household buildings, were perfect transmitters of the illness, as it was not in fact them, that spread the pandemic directly. The disease carriers were hidden in rats' fur, as well as in the coats of all other animals, and even in human hair – fleas and lice. The abundance and ubiquity of rats meant the same for the parasitic insects. Infected with bacteria, they were the real cause of the most fatal outbreak in the history of mankind, though still, even today, people tend to treat rats as the main source of this disaster. We also seem to forget that many factors inducted by humans fuelled the disease, like lack of hygiene, overpopulation in main cities, and poverty.

As a species we unintentionally helped rats, and greatly contributed to their conquest of the whole world. In fact, we did them a favor, at the same time shooting ourselves in the foot, by constructing a ship. Our curiosity and search for lands and material goods pushed us across the oceans and seas. Rats gladly ceased the opportunity to travel around the world with us as stowaways, in ships filled up with tempting food ratios. New lands meant new possibilities not only for people, but also for these little critters. Both of our species rapidly increased the population, thriving in new environments. And as we aimed for the same shores, the war was getting more fierce.

Rodents have always been present in our lives. As we were reaching for higher standards of living, rats and mice did the same. At some point, our comfort has been disrupted by these little creatures, and we just wanted them gone. The truth is, we had plenty of time to master many varied methods of fighting rats and mice. Our ancestors domesticated cats, the biggest enemies of all rodents. Specially bred dogs followed, to hunt all animals being a nuisance for mankind. The development of snap traps added a lethal weapon to our arsenal. Agonizing and painful death from injuries, starvation, dehydration or exhaustion caused by jaw or glue traps is what we have served these animals.

Rodenticides boom during the 20th century brought even more suffering. Rat poison is one of the most common current weapons against these animals, causing internal bleeding by preventing the body from recycling vitamin K, needed to clot blood. Hemorrhage can last a few days before the animal dies. Death is painful and slow. Squirrels, birds, domestic cats and dogs, owls, foxes and wolves are in danger of secondary or even tertiary poisoning. The rat dies, but the poison stays in its body and gets into other organisms that feed on the deceased.

Each day these little critters have to fight for their lives. Not only are they at the end of a food chain, but also most wanted by people. Rats pay a very high price for living among us. Their only crime is the fact that they have perfectly adapted to the environment completely transformed and ruled by humans.

Surprisingly, the great effort from our side to eradicate these rodents in fact came to nought, as rats seem to be doing quite fine, with billions of individuals on six continents. Intelligent, agile, tough, very social and even empathetic – these critters were able to survive and spread their empire almost all around the globe, against all odds.

Coming back to the times of the Plague, the expan‹ population, caused by benefits of living among people, requi‹ radical steps from our side. Feeling threatened by the steadily growing number of these critters in European cities, a demand for a method to solve the problem rose in the communities. That is when a new job emerged – a rat catcher. It was most common for men from lower class to take up such jobs, as the risk of bites and infections was very high. Rodents stayed hidden in the manholes, haystacks, old buildings, and in dark locations, often with limited access to them. For that reason sometimes the only way to reach the animals was by putting a bare hand into slots and holes. Later poisons and traps have been invented to help with the extermination of the rats, and reduced the risk of direct contact. During social events and meetings on market squares rat catchers proudly presented their equipment to people, using it on caged rats and showing animals dying in agony to passers-by.

To improve their efficiency of hunting, and minimize the risk of being bitten, rat-catchers started to use the help of animals bred especially to kill rodents – so called "ratters". The development of small, agile kinds of dogs happened quickly, and terriers became quite a popular sight in the streets of big cities.

Soon rat catchers have found yet another way of using their companions, that could bring them a profit. A bloody gambling sport called rat baiting. Captive rodents were placed in an enclosed area, secured with wires or nails, preventing them from escaping. After the dog had been let in, the massacre began, to the spectators' delight. It was possible to win a great sum of money by betting on the fastest rattler, or estimating the amount of victims it would eliminate in a certain amount of time.

The demand for this entertainment grew so much that organizers started to breed rats on a massive scale to be able to provide the viewers with a bloody show. Ironically, it contributed to the increase of rodent number once again, as some animals were able to escape, and started to live on the streets. There is even an assumption that some rat catchers released rats bred in captivity on the street on purpose, to have more contracts and earn more money. It seems that people can turn every suffering into profitable business.

Surprisingly, there was one positive effect of the emergence of this peculiar profession. With millions of escaped rats swarming in cities, there was quite a big chance to find and catch extraordinarily colored individuals. Instead of being killed, those lucky ones were exhibited as unique creatures. Some rich and extravagant people desired to have them in their houses as pets, and thereby laid a foundation for domestication of rats. But the real breakthrough happened far away from European countries.

Timid steps of taming rats did not change the opinion most people had about them, especially in countries greatly affected by the Black Death. Meantime, in the East, the perceiving of these critters started to change slightly, together with their domestication, pioneered in Japan around the 18th century. During the Edo period it became popular, or even fancy, to keep rats as pets. The first guidebook about raising such extraordinary home critters was written in 1775 (*Yoso-tama-no-kakehashi*) and was followed by another one (*Chinganso-date-gusa*) twelve years later. They contained advice on how to breed rats in order to obtain the desired type. The Japanese started this procedure on a massive scale to obtain unusual coat colors (for example albino rat) and patterns (hooded rat), using the information included in the books. They initiated the emergence of so-called *fancy rats*, whose transformation continued in the United States and Europe, after the spread of pet rats on other continents. Further experiments with breeding resulted in appearance of different markings, coat types, colors, or even ear shape.

Domestication of rats shaped yet another group of these critters – laboratory rats. Albino rats emerged as a product of breeding hooded ones, and in 19th

century have been widely used for scientific purposes. They have contributed greatly to the development of many medicines, cancer treatment, behavioral research and many more experiments, but it earned them a life of suffering and pain. Even today rats are used for many cruel practices like testing of cosmetics, shock therapies, vivi sections and pain inflicting transplantations.

Each years millions of rats are bred and used in laboratories only to be euthanized after finished experiments or being the result of breeding surplus. Albino rats have white fur and characteristic red eyes, caused by the lack of the pigment which obscures the red blood cells visible in the retina. Therefore, they are more sensitive to light. Their eyesight is rather poor, and almost all albino rats lose it completely once they get older. But in fact, it does not make their life harder. Rats rely mostly on other senses like smell or touch, via whiskers, and even blind ones can move around excellently and live comfortably.

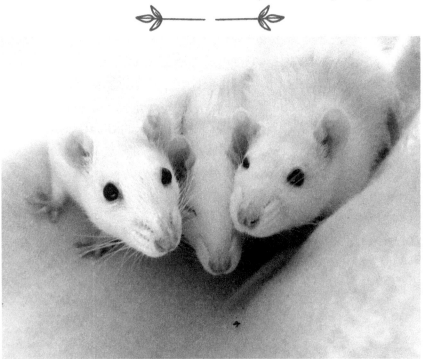

FIRST PUREBRED RATS

The love for purebred rodents started with the National Mouse Club, established in 1895 in England by Walter Maxey. The organization affiliated mice lovers and was organizing shows, publishing articles about mice, and teaching about their lifestyle and needs. These tiny creatures were selectively bred for exhibition and creation of new color species – sparking off fancy mice.

In 1901, a woman named Mary Douglas wanted to take part in the exhibition organized by NMC, but her candidate was not a mouse, it was her beloved hooded rat. Nonetheless, the permission was granted and soon, to the surprise of all contestants, it won the show. England fell in love with fancy rats and the positive feedback resulted in changing the name of the institution for National Mouse and Rat Club. Mary gained the title of Mother of Rats. The grouping thrived, allying fans of mice and rats together, until Mary's death in 1920. During the next few years the popularity of fancy rats diminished, and the Club again focused only on mice. Though, once more rats came back to being mainly pests, rather than pets, their Mother sowed the seed of doubt in the society. She taught people that these animals can be very grateful and amazing pets. Her actions made people wonder if torturing them in labs and eliminating them on streets was just and right.

Despite a more favorable approach towards these animals in the beginning of the 20th century, fancy rats had to wait many more years before getting truly back to peoples' graces.

Even though several attempts to create clubs for their fans were initiated, it was not successful until 1976, when National Fancy Rat Society was founded in the United Kingdom. It was the first to focus solely on rats. Interest in these rodents rose once again, and new varieties have been bred and standardized. As more rat clubs started to be founded worldwide, the demand for more unique and exotic specimens rose, and once again rats traveled around the globe. But this time not hidden under the deck, like their wild cousins, but in comfortable and safe conditions, as valuable goods.

VARIETIES OF RATS

Over many years of selective breeding numerous varieties of rats have been created.

Today we can distinguish them based on few factors:

BODY TYPE

DUMBO

In the United States the idea to breed a rat that looks cuter emerged. Finally, individuals with large and round ears, set low down on the sides of the head, were born. Thanks to their appearance they were often compared to Disney's elephant Dumbo, hence the name of the variety.

Dumbo variety

MANX

Playing with genes resulted also in emergence of Manx rats, which are born without a tail. Perfect representatives of this variety have round rump and cobby bodies. Unfortunately, sometimes pups can be born with deformed, stub or limp tail, causing significant complications. More common health problems concern issues with bladder, proper development of feet, spine, or hind bones like pelvis. That is why breeding manx rats raises a lot of ethical questions.

HAIR TYPE

By inbreeding rats with extraordinary types of hair, few varieties have been created. Some of them had silky coats with lustrous sheen like *Satin*, some wavy, like *Velveteen*, or even curly, characteristic for *Rex*.

Rex variety

Due to mutations caused by further breeding, the lack of fur started to occur. This feature is visible in *Double-Rex*, *Fuzz* and *Sphynx* varieties. While the first type lacks mainly patches of hair, and the next has only little, peach-hair like fur, *Sphynx* rats do not have any single hair on their bodies.

Double-Rex variety

But messing with Mother Nature is always a bad idea. Furless rats are very susceptible to tumors and respiratory system diseases. They easily get cold and scratched. They need a diet rich in fat and protein, because they burn more calories than their furry friends, trying to keep their bodies warm.

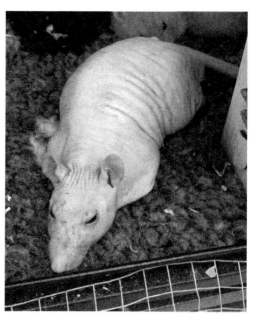

Fuzz variety

EYE COLOR

Most rats have black eyes, but sometimes their color may differ. When under the light they show a red glow – we are dealing with *ruby eyes*. Albino rats have *red* or *pink eyes*, regardless of the light, due to the lack of melanin pigment. Such eyes are sometimes

Pink-eyed albino variety

also characteristic for beige, grey or any other light color coat. Very rarely we can meet so called *odd-eyed* rats, with two eyes in different colors.

COAT

Rats can be classified not only due to their color, but also the pattern created by hairs.

When the whole body has one color, it is called a Self variety. Next to standard colors like black, white or beige, we can find for example soft-gray coated Russian Blue, with metallic sheen, light gray Platinum or rich and warm brown Chocolate type.

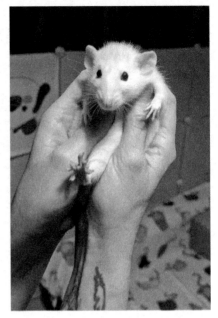

Odd-eyed variety

Self variety black rat

Russian Blue variety

Platinum variety

The legacy of rats' wild cousins, *Agouti* color, is a great example of *AOC – any other color* – variety. The coat consists of hairs of different colors, evenly interspersed with each other. Other examples of this type are

Agouti variety

Chinchilla, with different shades of gray, varying from black to white hair mixed together, creamy *Pearl*, golden *Fawn* with silver guard hair, or *Cinnamon*, having a combination of warm brown, grey and chocolate hair. When the coat consist of white guard hairs, variety is described as *Silvered*, including golden-white *Amber*, dove gray *Silver Lilac* or *Silvered Chocolate*.

Fawn variety

Rats with more than one color, creating a certain pattern, are standardized as *AOCP - any other color pattern*. Their body has one color, with darker spots, usually found near their muzzle and tail, like *Siamese*, beige with dark fur around mentioned areas, or *Himalayan*, white with dark nose. Both the varieties can have either black or red eyes. But some

Siamese variety

26

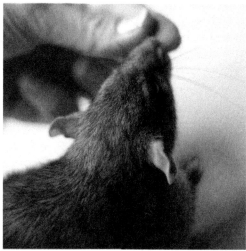

Himalayan variety

Burmese variety

have patches of differently colored hair all around the body, like toffee brown *Burmese*.

The biggest number of varieties can be found in a group called *Marked*. Patterns, created with colors on the rodent's coat, enable to categorize them as one of following types:

- *Bareback* - has a hood in different color, covering head, throat, chest and shoulders.
- *Berkshire* - with white belly and chest, distinctly separated from the top in any other color.
- *Blaze* - has a white spot, in the shape of wedge, that

Blaze variety

runs from muzzle to ears.

- *Capped rat* - clean white with only colored stain on head, reaching ears and jaw, which should stay white.
- *Dalmatian* - has splashes of color over all body.
- *Down Under* - characterized by colored spots and stripes on the belly with the same pattern or solid color on the back.
- *Essex* - color is most intense on the spine, gradually fading towards the belly, which is white.
- *Hooded* - has color similar to bareback type, but the hood spot runs over the spine, through the whole body.
- *Husky* – color resembles the one from popular dog's breed – dark gray back, gradually fading into white belly and muzzle.
- *Irish* - distinguished by a triangle white spot on the chest, covering also front paws.
- *Masked* - pure white body, with only one spot

Hooded variety

28   *Husky variety*

on the face, just around the eyes.

- Variegated - has many spots on their body, the biggest on the head and shoulders and small ones covering the rest of the body.

Mentioned varieties does not mean that rats cannot occur in any other color or pattern of fur. These are types standardized by Rat Associations, but they also can vary in different countries. Nonetheless, the above plurality of types shows how, through selective breeding, people were able to affect not only the color but also structure of rat's fur or shape of the body. Rats finally managed to take part in exhibitions, gain titles, win prizes and share their unique genes with other generations. From sewers they raised to podiums and exclusive ratteries to become fancy rats, cutting off from their wild, dun cousins.

ARE YOU READY FOR THIS ADVENTURE?

Knowing some basic facts about rats, now it is time to explore the secrets of caring for these fantastic creatures. It is also a time to answer yourself this one important question, are you ready for this adventure?

Before the decision is made, all cons and pros should be reviewed. Rats are fascinating and grateful animals, bringing a lot of joy and love, but they also require a lot of attention and time. Below are some topics, every future rat owner should consider:

1. The golden rule is – you cannot keep only one rat. There is no excuse like – I do not have enough space, I do not have enough money, I do not want more than one pet. If so – choose another critter that leads solitary life, like a hamster or male mouse (keep in mind that guinea pigs, rabbits and female mice – just

like rats - must have a companion of its own species!). For rats, having a companion is as important as having food and water. They will not die from loneliness – though there are cases, when after the death of one rat, the health of the second deteriorated, leading to its passing – but they can suffer mentally. Imagine living your life not knowing any other human. Physically you can manage on your own, but your psyche will not be in a good shape. And no, no other animal, not even you, can replace another rat. Only in extreme situations can a rat be kept on its own, when a vet decides so, due to the rat's sickness, or when you are left with one eldery rat.

2. Rats are really vulnerable to a lot of diseases. Most of them suffer from cancerous tumors, or have various problems with the respiratory system in their adult life. The treatment can be very expensive and visits at the veterinary clinic quite frequent. Most of the institutions do not have the medical equipment adjusted to the size of a rat, or some vets simply lack the knowledge of treating rodents. That is why it is essential to find a clinic that specializes in little animals. To avoid tumors, which can grow surprisingly rapidly, rats should be neutered, best at the age of few months – both females and males. It is yet another expense a rat owner must prepare for. Moreover, such a procedure should be executed under inhalation anesthesia, which is not available in every clinic and may be more expensive.

3. Rats are very active animals and require quite a lot of exercise. Their cage should be big enough and properly adapted to their needs (you will find information on how to prepare a perfect cage later in the book). What is more, is it necessary for these critters to be able to run in the open, outside the cage at least for an hour per day – what creates another problem we will have to face while keeping a rat – a safe and spacious place in the house to let our little friends frolic.

4. Before adopting a rat we should also consider who will take care of our pet when we are not at home. It will be the biggest challenge especially in the time of summer vacations. Rats can stay alone in the house for two or three days – of course with the proper amount of food and water left – but not longer. They also should not travel far distances, because it generates a lot of stress, so taking them with you while traveling is a bad idea.

If you are planning a longer vacation, ask your friends or members of the family to watch over your rats, or find a place, like a hotel for animals, where you can leave them. Try to look on fan forums or social media groups for private individuals, who offer services as rodents caretakers. Some good souls will gladly take care of your pets just for a bottle of wine or a pack of cookies. You can also buy a camera through which you can observe your pets when you are out, via your mobile phone.

5. Rats are very social, not only when it comes to the rest of their mischief, but also people. They are not the type of animals that can spend most of the day in a cage and just eat, drink and sleep. They need interaction with people. Taking care of rats requires time and engagement, so if you prefer to spend your free time outside the house – better think about a different pet.

If you still think you can own one rat and keep it happy, once again I will repeat myself, you can not.
Why? Let me explain briefly.
The needs of animals can be divided into non-elastic and elastic ones. These first are needs, which must be fulfilled in order to keep an animal alive. They relate to the physical wellbeing of a creature and lack of them leads to death. Starting from basic ones like food and water, it also includes sleep and the feeling of safety.
Elastic needs differ more than non-elastic ones for certain species of animals. They mostly cover the need for movement (for example parrots have a need to fly, ducks to swim, etc.), mental stimulation, need of reproduction and, in the case of animals living naturally in groups, need of social life. The fact that neglecting them will not cause death directly, does not make them less important for proper operation of an organism. They have a huge influence on animal's mental health, development and comfort of life.

Though dogs, just as rats, are very social animals, they can be kept solo, thanks to their domestication, which started around 25 000 years ago. During all this time dogs adjusted to living among people. According to some behaviorists – they even treat us like members of their pack. It does not mean that they do not need contact with other dogs – of course, it is also essential for them, but not constantly. Meetings with other animals of the same species influence an individual's mental health, provide important information, stimulation, and opportunity to play and learn. The domestication of rats is dated only to the beginning of the XVIII century, so relatively recently. They also are not able to interact with us the same way dogs can, so they need a group made up of individuals of their own species. No other living creature is able to replace another rat.

As people, we also count as social creatures. Even when you are an extreme introvert can you imagine a life without any other human? Without your family or friends? With no one to talk to, to get support from, to learn, play as a child, share your life with?

With the source of food and sweet water you could survive alone, but without a doubt your mental health would be in very bad shape.

People tend to create excuses for keeping a sole rat, guinea pig or chinchilla – we complain we do not have a proper cage, or enough money to buy a bigger one. We cannot afford a vet, there is too little time, our parents do not want to agree for more than just one pet. I was such a person in the past. But I quickly learnt that this approach is irresponsible and selfish.

I meet people claiming that they will take such good care of their animal, that it will not need company of their own species. Nothing more wrong. Though interspecies friendship is possible, no other animal will replace a friend of the same breed. The conclusion is simple – rats need the companionship of other rats to lead a happy and healthy life. If we are unable to meet their natural needs, we should think about other pets. What is the point of keeping an unhealthy and miserable animal? If it is only for our fun and amusement, then it is very cruel and counts as mistreatment. We are responsible for what we have tamed. Not only for our animals' physical health but also mental one.

WHERE TO GET A RAT FROM?

While thinking about obtaining a new pet, the first place that comes to our mind is – petstore. Unfortunately, this is a very bad idea. Why? Because this kind of business, selling living creatures on a mass scale, is a cradle of suffering. Let's take a closer look at what a petshop really is. This is a place where anybody (even a child) can buy a pet, a living and feeling creature, for only a few coins, and without any check of the future conditions of its living. For the shop, this animal is only a merchandise, which is meant to be sold and bring profit. Some of you may feel offended now – after all many pet shops have very experienced staff and great conditions. But what is common for all establishments of this kind? They trade, so they are profit oriented, not animal welfare oriented. The more they sell, the more they earn.

Let's dig deeper. Every store must have a supplier – so a company which produces certain goods and carries out wholesale. And production is an adequate word for this process, even in the case of animals. Let's suppose a rat costs 10 $ in a petstore. The margin, so an additional cost imposed on a "commodity" in order to sell for more than it has been bought, can reach up to 40%. It means that the supplier sells it for only a few dollars per animal. Just imagine how many pets have to be sold to obtain a rational profit. It all comes to one question – what were the conditions of bringing up an animal when it can be sold so cheap? The answer is often unpleasant and cruel, as we are dealing with mass breeding, where the main idea is to produce as many *goods* as possible, as cheaply as possible. Rats, guinea pigs, rabbits and all other animals available at pet shops are usually kept in small cages or even plastic boxes, fed low-cost and low-quality food, unattended by any vet, and their only goal is to multiply. Females are often exhausted by being forced to give birth each time they are fertile. Inbreeding is very common in such pet factories, which results in the occurrence of many diseases that are later passed from generation to generation. As most of the health problems occur at a later age, the small cute critters seem perfectly fine through the glass of the shop window.

Coming back to our supply chain - when our *merchandise* reaches the store, it has to be put into some kind of a container. Usually it is made of glass, so the *commodity* is perfectly visible for customers, and at the same time – totally exposed to light, noise and chaotic movement in the store. Often these animals do not have any place to hide from the light or human eye, no shady, dark place to rest, sleep, or just have a little privacy. Pet stores located in shopping malls are disclosed to unnatural light during days and night, constant noise, and loud sounds. Exposed to all these factors, animals are just stressed. The containers are often also too small, even if, in theory, they are just temporary. Additionally, they have bad air flow and are not cleaned on a regular basis, so many of them are quickly filled with fumes of ammonia from the urine. Some shops do not have air conditioning, what also affects animals, depriving them from any place to cool their bodies, or warm them during cold seasons, when the heating in the facility is turned off after working hours.

Many newly arrived babies are taken from their mothers too early. Often one litter lands in the same container, no matter the sex. There is a high chance of unknowingly buying a pregnant rat. The problem is that these animals reproduce without any supervision, between siblings, and no matter the health issues. A lot of animals bought in pet shops have lice or fleas, being a consequence of bad hygiene, lack of proper living conditions, and veterinary supervision.

It is tempting to have an opportunity to choose a young, cute rat from a petstore, which is available basically any time. Easy, quick, cheap – but also cruel.

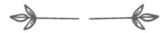

Personally, I avoid buying anything in stores that sell living creatures. Food, substrate, accessories or toys – I get it only via the Internet or in stationary shops, which do not have animals on their list of goods.
It does not matter if you buy a pet, a cage, or a pack of grains, your money goes to a shop supporting mass breeding. Demand drives supply.

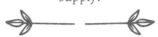

For me, personally, the best way to obtain a rat (or any other pet) is to adopt it. We all are aware of shelters or charities that look for homes for cats and dogs, most of us have heard about societies rescuing horses or farm animals, but unfortunately still, such organizations helping rodents – rats, mice, hamsters etc. - are a big surprise for a large percentage of the society.

These small animals are mostly saved from bad conditions in shops or private individuals' houses. Some of them are collected from streets, tossed out like trash, or from people who are no longer able to take care of them. Many rat lovers run foster houses privately, where they take care of unwanted, homeless pets. But before an animal is handed to you, in most cases you need to sign an adoption questionnaire prepared by a charity or foster home. It contains questions about food, cage, vet care, your experience with these critters and similar inquiries. Pre-adoption visits are also commonly organized. This means that a volunteer can come to your house to evaluate the conditions the animal will live in. These people will simply talk to you, give you some advice, they are always helpful and open to questions, as the animal's welfare is in their best interest. It may seem troublesome, even uncomfortable for some people, but this is the best way to check the future home, and it is worth it to spare a while in order to rescue the life of some little creature.

Do not be discouraged if the foster house or charity is far away from you – there are many groups on social media that help with animal transportation. You can easily find somebody who travels through your country and will agree to take one extra passenger.

In many cases the adoption means a life for animals. In Poland, there is a charity that saves rats, mice, rabbits, and cavies used in laboratories. These creatures are after not invasive experiments, or from breeding surplus. After they serve their purpose - they are put down, as such facilities do not have a possibility to take care of all these animals. Adopting them means saving their lives.

If, for any reason, you are forced to give up on your rat – do not give it back to the pet store or, what's worse – do not release it into the wild! Some people think that all animals can survive outside – which is very disturbing, and indicates a total lack of basic knowledge. By doing so, we are basically passing a death sentence on a creature. Domestic rats, rabbits, mice, or any other animals raised in captivity, are not able to adapt to the conditions of living in the outside world. Abandoned pets will certainly die during the first few days, usually from starvation or thirst, hypothermia, or sickness. Many of them will be killed by another animal, car or even human.

If you really do not have the possibility to keep your pet any longer, try to find another home for the critter. There are a lot of groups on social media, where people will help you look for a new owner, you can always ask charities or foster houses for help.

CAGE

Rats need a cage that is properly fitted for their needs. They cannot live in the aquarium or any other glass or plastic container. Their house must be airy and spacious, as they are very active and energetic animals. Their urine is rich in nitrogen, forming ammonia while breaking down in the presence of oxygen, which gives rat's pee a very strong odor. It also can be harmful in high density, that is why the proper air flow in the cage is essential.

The cage cannot have less than 31 inches in length and height, and 20 inches in width. Such one can accommodate from two to four rats. The more rats we are planning to have or

already have, the bigger their house must be. The cage should be higher rather than longer – to create shelves for rats to climb on. Be sure to check if the space between bars is small enough, so the rats will not squeeze throught.

If you are looking for a cage, I strongly recommend you to buy it on the Internet. Nowadays, there are a lot of models already adapted to the needs of critters of all kinds. Quite often stationary pet shops do not have proper cages, and tend to recommend not suitable accommodations. Moreover, the price difference can be quite significant.

Now, when we have a proper cage, we need to furnish it. In the wild, rats have many enemies that can attack from the ground and the air. That is why they avoid open areas and prefer dark, narrow places to hide inside, or to climb on, just to feel safe. The same is with our home pets – the cage cannot be empty, we need to provide hideouts, hammocks, ladders etc. There is an abundance of beautiful accessories, like sewn houses or blankets for critters available. Just remember that we are dealing with rodents, who have a need of chewing and biting, so do not get angry when the next day everything will be torn to pieces and destroyed. Rats' teeth can easily cut through a brick, so

materials like cloth or plastic are not a challenge for them. If you want a cheap alternative, I recommend hammocks and tunnels from sleeves of old blouses, trousers, or a hat as a sleeping bag. Just remember to choose safe materials without loose threads – like knitted jumpers – as they can tangle around rat's paws and claws.

houses and caves, in which rats can hide, store food, or build nests, are yet another great cage enrichment . They come in different sizes, colors, and are made from many materials. Though it may seem that a wooden house is a good idea – believe me, it is not. A lot of rats have a tendency to pee just when and where they feel the urge. Wood easily absorbs the urine, and the smell can be unbearable. The same goes with wooden floors – they are not practical, as they need to be often replaced when dirty. Plastic houses and platforms make a better alternative, they are cheaper and easier to clean.

Cardboard boxes are a great material to build houses for rats. Joining boxes together, cutting holes in them, or making tunnels can lead to the creation of real rat cardboard castles. One disadvantage is that it easily absorbs liquids, and is very tempting for rats to chew on, so it is not very durable.

Rats adore narrow, tight hideouts. We can provide them with such attractions by installing tunnels in the cage. It is possible to buy accessories dedicated to critters, but a piece of plastic pipe is also a good idea. Just be sure that your rat will not get stuck in it! Use the legs of old trousers to make hung tunnels for your pets. It gives them an opportunity not only to hide, but also climb.

To provide a diverse

and interesting environment for rats, you can also put inside the cage some items like branches of fruit trees, climbing ladders, boxes for example with torn pieces of tissues, sand for animals, or just old pieces of cloth for rats to dig in. Remember that whatever you put in the cage needs to be clean and safe.

Leaving the plastic bottom of the cage empty can result in a smelly and dirty outcome. Rats pee quite often, and it is recommended to fill the cage with absorbent substrate. The most common, unfortunately, seems to be the wooden shavings of sawdust. Often it is filled with a lot of dust and wood particles, which inhaled by the animal, cause respiratory system problems, or even allergies. Be sure to always look for the ones, which are dust-free.

Hay is not suitable for rats. Pointy ends of blades can damage an animal's eyes or mouth, some can be infested with lice or other small insects. Additionally, it creates a good environment for bugs and parasites to develop, when wet with urine.

Pellets are much safer but, once again, we have to pay attention to the details.

One of the cheapest and most common pellets is made of pine. Keep in mind that conifer trees are toxic to rats, as so is the bedding made from them. Phenol contained in pine may smell nice, but may also cause intoxication when inhaled. This, in turn, leads to the destruction of cells in lungs. Contact with the skin also endangers rat's health. The organism constantly tries to get rid of the toxins, stressing the liver.

Pellets made of corn cobs are also not recommended. When swallowed, it gets moldy and can lead to choking.

Choosing a pellet for your rats, aim for the one made of hemp, paper, straw or non toxic deciduous trees.

Beech chips are quite effective when it comes to absorbing

liquids, they are natural and safe.

We can also line the bottom with bathroom mat or blanket, though it requires regular washing.

Avoid any chemical cat substrates! Choose only natural materials, as sometimes rats can nibble on the pellet.

Rapid rodent metabolism leads to the production of a big amount of waste. For this reason, cleaning of the cage should be done regularly, to decrease the chance of infection and diseases caused by the lack of hygiene. In fact, rats are very clean animals, despite their reputation. They use their little tongues to take care of their fur, as well as other's members of the group. Most of them defecate in one place. That is why creating a litter box can help us maintain a clearer cage, and make tidying easier. The learning process can take some time but is worth the effort.

Put the litter box in one of the corners of the cage, as such areas are often used as a toilet. It is helpful to fill it with a different substrate than is used in the rest of the cage, for example when rats have a mat in a cage, let's use a pellet inside a litter box. And now, the hard part – collect the droppings from all over the cage, and put them in the litter box. It will encourage animals to use it as a toilet next time they feel the urge. If one rat succeeds, there is a great chance that the rest will imitate the behavior.

While cleaning the litter box, as well as a whole cage, do not use chemical detergents, as they are harmful for rats. There are special cleaning products safe for animals, but you can as well use water with a drop of vinegar, or natural and ecological dish soap.

TOYS

Like many other domestic pets, rats love playing with toys. Keeping them entertained makes them happy at the same time. Aside from providing wellbeing support, toys stimulate animals mentally and physically, bond the mischief together, and relieve stress. You can put some playthings inside a cage, but have most of them ready for the time rats spend outside the cage. It keeps them busy and provides challenges. In pet stores you can find a variety of toys for rodents – just avoid the ones painted or made from toxic materials. Below are a few propositions of toys that are most frequently used by my rats.

-Interactive toys for dogs, snuffle mats or puzzles, can keep your rats entertained for a long time, and stimulate them mentally.

-Balls with a hole – fill them with tasty treats and let the rolling begin.

-Balls from natural materials – made from straw or branches, provide a great opportunity to chase and chew.

-Fishing rods for cats – not only felines adore chasing after rustling, running objects.

-Table tennis balls – the smooth surface makes it impossible for a rat to grab, so the chase can be endless. Unless, some clever rat manages to bite it.

-Ropes and hammocks – you can also install them outside the cage, to provide your rats with a chance of climbing.

Never buy a spinning wheel for your rats. It can hurt their backs, by bending the body unnaturally, and damage or even break the tail, which can easily get stuck between the bars. Hamster balls are also a bad idea, not only for rats,

but rodents in general. They make animals anxious or even frightened, as critters are literally stuck in a very limited area. The air flow is bad, so it quickly gets stuffy inside. Moreover, the sense of direction of an animal is disturbed. In fact, our pet is just mindlessly running forward. As a result, the ball can easily get stuck, bump into many objects, or fall from the stairs.

With a tendency to bite, and a curious nature, the need of replacing rats' toys can occur quite often. *Do It Yourself* toys can be a good solution. They are easy to make, and can be as entertaining as the ones from the store.

-Digging box – cut the top of the box and make a hole for rats to enter. Fill the box with pieces of torn tissue, paper or material, add some sunflower or pumpkin seeds, nuts, pieces of fruit and stir the content. Your pets will have great fun digging for treats.

-Cardboard castle – use boxes to build a construction with holes, extra floors, labyrinths, and tunnels.

-Toilet paper roll toy – bend the edge of a toilet paper roll to close one end, fill it with treats and close the second end the same way.

-Toilet paper ball – cut toilet paper roll into rings. Slide one on another to create a ball, and fill with treats.

-Christmas cracker – fill a toilet paper roll with treats, and wrap it into a paper, just like a cracker. Your rats will have to use their heads to get to the treat.

-Pipe labyrinths – use plastic pipes and tunnels to create a great toy for your rat, filled with scattered treats.

-Digging site – take a blanket or a bigger piece of cloth, roll it over in one corner, fold in the second one, and wrinkle the rest in a way to create many sockets for treats. Your rats will have to find not only the food, but also a way to get to it.

-Swimming pool – remember to use it only when the temperature is adequate. Fill a plastic container with warm water. Be sure that its depth always allows rats to breathe the air, animal's feet need to touch the bottom! Put some green peas inside to enrich the fun. Prepare an absorbent towel to gently dry your rat when the playtime is over. Keep in mind that not all rats

57

like to get wet, so never force them to go inside the pool.

Taking a rat for a walk outside is not an entertainment for the animal. On the contrary, it makes the animal stressed, and scared. Our pet is in a new place, a vast open area which is frightening, unknown, and can make the rat react in an unpredictable way. Even if trained to sit on your shoulder, it can jump off, and hurt itself, run away or get attacked by other animals. Harnesses and leashes for critters are also useless, and do not ensure safety.
Domestic rats do not have a need to go outside of your home. As mentioned before, rats in general do not live in open areas. They hide, and are active mostly after dusk to avoid the sun. Let your rats roam your home instead, and explore a safe and controlled environment.

Keep your rats entertained to maintain their mental and physical health. Challenge their intellect, test their cleverness, and let them enjoy the tasty reward. You can even teach your rats many tricks, just like dogs - fetching, swirling or coming at call.

FOOD

Rats are omnivorous, which means that their diet must be properly balanced. Feral rats feed on whatever they can find, their stomach is very resistant. But our pets require a more healthy diet, if we want to keep them in good form and ensure a long life. Do not give them sweets, dinner leftovers, salty or spicy food. It will only deteriorate their health and damage internal organs. The iconic image of a rat with cheese has a detrimental effect on the perception of the diet of these rodents. Such products contain a lot of salt and should be avoided. I am also not a fan of videos on the Internet on which rats are given pancakes, sweets or chips, just to make them look cute or do a trick. People are often not aware of the effect the quantity of unhealthy food, which seems small for us, has on a little rodent's body. Do not make a trash bin out of your

pet's stomach, and do not fill it with leftovers. If you want to share a dinner with your rat, boil rice, grain or potatoes in water without salt, and add spices only to the dish you have on your plate.

Grains are the basis of the healthy nourishment, and should cover around 75-80% of the menu. Ready mixes are available in all pet shops, but be sure to always check the composition. You will certainly not find a good quality brand on a low price shelf. Invest in the healthy diet of your rat, as it will keep your little friend in good condition. Look for a forage with a great variety of seeds and grains, dried herbs and nuts. The ingredients should be natural.

Avoid puffed rice, baked, colorful crisps and granules.

Though they look attractive for us humans, their color indicates chemical, harmful composition. What is more, they often have little nutritional value. Raisins, which are usually artificially sweetened and sprayed during growing, and dried citrus are dangerous ingredients, evade them.

You can also compose your own mix for rats from nuts, sunflower and pumpkin seeds, dried peas, corn, wheat, fruits, and all kinds of grains. Then you have full control over your rats diet, though finding proper and varied ingredients can be time and money consuming.

Buy a package of seeds and nuts in shells – sunflower, pumpkin, peanut, walnut – and give it to your rat. Opening such tasty treats is a great activity for your pets, challenging and entertaining. Control the amount your rats eat per day, such products are high in fat!

Vegetables and fruits, rich in vitamins and minerals, should cover 5-20% of rats' diet. It is advised to give them every day, as a fresh meal. Try to diversify all types of food you give to your pets – the more varied the diet, the better. Almost all fruit and veggies are good for rats, but you should never give them :

* citrus - they can trigger problems with kidneys in male rats, though they are safe for females.

*onions - they are very toxic to rats. Their poisonous gas can lead to the suffocation of the animal.

*grapes from markets - they contain a lot of sugar.

*stones and pits fruits - most of them contain traces of a highly toxic chemical, called cyanide. That is why we should never feed rats apple cores and unpitted cherries, or other fruits.

*avocado seed and peel - they are toxic. The flesh is safe to be given to rats, but due to the high fat content, the amount should be limited.

*raw beans - contains toxic hemagglutinin.

*green bananas - they cause digestive problems.

*green potatoes - they contain solanine, which causes poisoning.

*Spinach - it can cause urinary problems, as well as

stones in kidneys and bladder.

Herbs can also be added to the diet, as they are a tasty and healthy snack. Buy dried mint, chamomile, plantain, oregano, basil or marjoram, or pick fresh ones from your garden or fields – just remember to choose places away from roads, as pollution from cars can contaminate the plants. Always be sure you know what herb you pick up!

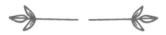

Collect seeds left by fussy rats and germinate them to grow a tasty and healthy treat.

As already mentioned before, rats are omnivorous, so small amounts of meat can also be included in their menu. Choose good quality poultry or beef – pork is too fat – and boil it without any salt or seasoning. Raw or fried meat is not advisable. Dried or alive mealworms are also very nutritious, and eagerly eaten by many rats.

Natural yogurt and cottage cheese can be served in small amounts, though I recommend it mostly for blending with medicine if needed. It should not be given daily.

You can also boil an egg (never serve raw one!), let it cool – remember that even when the shell is cold, the insides of the egg can still be very hot! – and give to your rats. It can be more fun if you just crack the shell a little bit, and let the rats peel the egg themselves. Just control the amount they eat, and always monitor your pets during the egg chase, as yolk can sometimes cause problems with swallowing, and lead to choking.

Remember to serve your pets only filtered water, never fluorinated or chlorinated one. Alcohol and sweetened drinks are also out of the question.

Prepare a tasty smoothie for your pets. Blend some fruits together, enrich it with herbs and a drop of honey, for sweet taste and immunity increasing properties. You can also add a little bit of peanut butter – but only if it is made 100% from nuts, or natural yogurt. Just be careful to not make it too sticky. Thick foods, like peanut butter, can cause choking.

Rats can not vomit, they are physically unable to do so. If you see your pet behave like it is going to throw up, it gasps for air, or nervously shakes its head, it is probably due to the choking. In such situations you must act quickly. Grab a rat, put your pointing fingers under the animal's neck, thumbs above it. Middle and ring fingers should secure the belly, while little fingers go behind hind paws. Lift the animal over your head, be sure that the grasp is steady (but not tight enough to crush your pet), and bring it down in a rapid arc. In the final stage, your rat should be placed tail up and head down. Repeat three times and give your pet time to rest. If there is no visible result, do the procedure once more. See if there is anything in the mouth, mucus or swollen object, remove it and wait till your friend feels better.

Paying attention to what our rats consume is essential. Food influences pets' health, well-being, gives them pleasure, entertainment, and fun.

Unfortunately, not all what lands in our animals' mouths is dedicated and safe for eating. While our rats act anemic, seem bloated or sensitive to touching the belly, it is often a consequence of swallowing something that should not be swallowed by our rodent. Do not underestimate the symptoms, and contact your vet. In such situations time is of the essence.

Unbalanced diet, genetic factors, environment, hormones, and gender, all of these factors have a great influence on rats' health. As most of them descend from individuals used in the lab, they carry the problems of their ancestors with them, and pass them to the future generations. This is a very important reason why the breeding of rats should be left only for experienced breeders, who can select healthy and suitable units to be parents, by monitoring the lineage.

TUMORS

One of the rats' most common health issues are tumors. These rodents have a tragic past, they suffered greatly, closed in laboratories used for decades as test animals. Some experiments included the deprivation of the immune system in order to grow, for example, a human ear under their skin. Other individuals had cancerous cells implemented into their bodies, which enabled the research on how the disease progresses. With a weakened immune system, passed down from generation to generation, caring for rats' health is a serious mission.

Two types of tumors can be distinguished – benign (non cancerous) and malignant (cancerous) ones. These first ones are less aggressive, and do not spread to other organs or parts of the body. They also create a membrane around them, separating the growth from nearby tissues, what makes them easier to remove. They are rather easy to detect under fingers, and usually grow rapidly, causing not only pain, problems with moving, climbing, or eating, but also internal damage. The lump growth causes pressure on vital organs, what in turn can lead to internal hemorrhage and eventually death. Sudden weight fluctuation is a clear sign that our rat should be examined by a vet. Some tumors grow so big that the animal is not able to eat enough to support its own organism and the growth. The sooner the treatment is implemented, the better chances of survival. In most cases the surgical removal of the lump allows an animal to go back to normal life. The age of a rat is also significant. The older the rat, the lesser the chance of safe awakening from anesthesia. Do not wait until

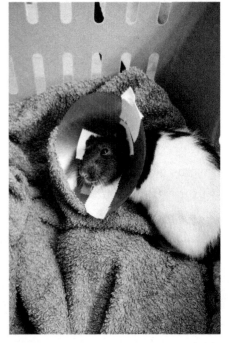

the tumor grows. Contact your vet the very moment you find something worrying in the behavior, or look of your rat.

Malignant tumors are more aggressive and dangerous. They can attack and invade nearby tissues or even different parts of the body. They often cause the failure of organs and lead to changes in behavior – problems with basic functioning of the organism, such as eating or moving, lack of response for outside impulses, or lethargy.

Some tumors cannot be removed, mostly due to their location. Brain, pituitary, or Zymbal's gland tumors are inoperable, but with the help of a proper medicine, their growth can be stopped or slowed down.

To decrease the probability of a tumor to occur, we should avoid high-calorie products in our rats' diet, and protect our pets from environmental toxins like tobacco smoke or chemical fumes, which weakens the immune system. Neutering both, males and females, significantly reduces the chances of the disease, best performed around six month of age. Tumors affected by hormones develop rapidly after rat's menopause, which happens when the animal is 18 months old.

Neutering female rats prevents not only the appearance of tumors, but also pyomixia (infection of the womb), which can lead to the animal's death. The pus fills the reproductive organs, causing stomach bloat, or leaks outside, together with blood, giving off unpleasant smell. Other symptoms include lack of appetite, excessive drinking and peeing, or weakness.

LUNG AND AIRWAY DISORDERS

Rats often suffer from respiratory system diseases. One of the most common is mycoplasmosis, usually caused by infectious agents called *Mycoplasma pulmonis*. It is very hard to treat, and in most cases often relapses. The disease impairs the ability of the airways to properly clean themselves, additionally creating an opportunity for other infections to quickly develop.

Mycoplasmosis is very contentious. Most rats bought from pet stores are the carriers of this disease, mostly due to the conditions in such facilities, poor diet, stress, overcrowding, and lack of treatment in the early stage. If one animal falls sick, the whole group catches the infection. Even the next rodents placed in the same container can get Mycoplasmosis.

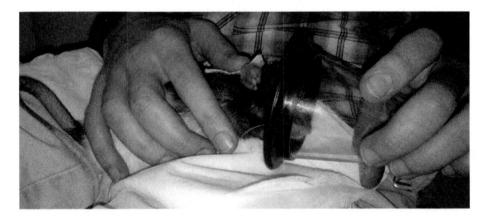

Mycoplasmosis is transmitted through direct contact between rats. Alarming signs are sneezing, head tilting, nasal discharge, wheezing, and rattling. Red tears (chromodacryorrhea) or stains around the nose indicates airway disorder, but also other diseases or stress. It is a clear sign that your companion needs an examination from the vet. Without a fast treatment, a sick rat starts to breathe by the mount, drool excessively and choke, as the infection moves from the upper part of the respiratory system to the lower one, attacking lungs.

Though a sick rat can look like it is crying blood, in fact the liquid coming out of its eyes and nose is called porphyrin. It is produced by a gland located in the eye's orbit, called the Harderian gland.

Rats are prone to many other viral or bacterial diseases. To protect your pets from respiratory system disorders, always pay attention to the signs animals give you. Time is of the essence when it comes to treatment. Additionaly, avoid drafts in the room the cage is in. Always remember about quarantine for a new member of the group, as such diseases spread rapidly. It is easier to cure one rat than the whole mischief.

PARASITES

Parasites can attack from both sides, from inside and outside. Fur is often their ideal environment, and can be infected with fleas, lice, and scabies. First signs are excessive scratching, red skin, little wounds, and small bald spots on the body. The transmission of the parasites is very easy, as they can transport themselves from one individual to another. On the contrary, getting rid of them can take a long time. After a vet recommends a proper treatment, the whole cage must be sterilized to get rid of parasites and their eggs. Moreover, setting stricter rules of hygiene is required.

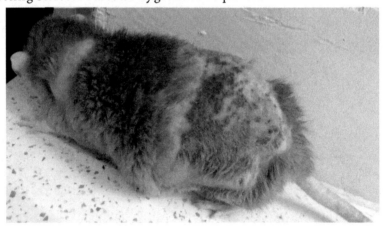

Most common intestinal parasites are pinworms. Infected rats can suffer from diarrhea, weight loss, and lack of appetite. Intensified licking of the rectal area often indicates the presence of these parasites. Such behavior is also characteristic with tapeworm infection. Parasites or their eggs are often present in feces, so when you notice any symptoms in one individual, the whole pack requires a visit at the vet's.

FUNGAL INFECTIONS

Scratching, red pimples, and balding are typical symptoms not only for parasites, but also fungal infection. A vet can take a sample of scraped skin for analysis and implement a proper treatment. One method of getting rid of fungal infections includes bathing in proper medicines. Keep in mind that this is the only exception when we should give our rat a bath.
There is no need to bathe a healthy rat, they can take care of their hygiene themselves.

PODODERMATITIS

The inflammation of the skin of the paw is predominantly caused by too hard bedding, wet and dirty substrate, or wire-floored cages. Secure horizontal bars of the cage with drybed, rug or cardboard. Walking on bars is not only painful, but also uncomfortable, and can lead to sprains of the limbs. The disease is very painful for rats, as they suffer with every step. Infested paws are red and can be swallowed or have ulcers on the bottom.

DENTAL DISEASES

All rodents' incisors grow continuously, so these animals need to systematically grind them. Improper positioning of teeth makes this process impossible, and can lead to many health problems, or even death. Overgrown incisors prevent rats from eating, causing starvation. When you notice that your rat avoids hard food, eats slowly and reluctantly, contact your vet. Checking the inside of your pet's muzzle is also a good habit, but keep in mind that not all dental problems are visible at the first sight.

Rat organism is fragile and prone to many diseases. It has to work very intensely in order to keep such a little body warm, what therefore leads to rapid development of many illnesses. They can be fatal without fast treatment. It is better safe than sorry, so always contact your vet when you see any worrying signs.

INTRODUCING RATS

The fact that rats are social creatures does not mean that they will always easily and gladly make friends with any other representative of their species. They are territorial animals, and can fiercely defend their home. Before any individual can join the mischief, a bond should be created between a newcomer and stationary rat. Sometimes it takes a few hours, sometimes weeks or even months. It all depends on the rat's personality – these rodents are born with some predispositions, some are more submissive, calm and friendly, some stubborn and dominant. Nonetheless, it is important to always prepare rats for a new company, and follow certain rules to avoid unpleasant situations. Our goal, as their keepers, is to conduct the introduction safely, as even calm and non-aggressive individuals can turn into troublesome rascals when confronted with a new tenant.

While introducing a new rat to a group, we have to remember a few basic rules. The most important one is to keep new pet, as well as stationary ones, safe. Of course we also have to remember about our safety as angry, stressed rats can be dangerous, and can cause very serious wounds. Most of the injuries heal, leaving no marks, sometimes smaller or bigger scars, but remember that rats' teeth are very strong and can damage not only the skin, but also the muscles or nerves in our body.

If you want to create mischief from female and male members, always remember to neuter at least one of the sexes before the introduction. While Adopting baby rats (at least four weeks old), we need to take into consideration their needs and specific behavior, characteristic of youngsters. It is best to adopt at least two young rats instead of one, especially when our mischief consists of older individuals. A company of active and fidgety babies can tire other rats, or even make them aggressive towards newcomers. When there are two babies they will play together and use most of their energy on each other, rather than bother seniors.

Coming to a new house, every animal needs some time to accommodate. Do not rush and, under any circumstances, do not let a new rat into the cage immediately, without any preparation. Be patient and observe the signals your rats give you, and everything should go smoothly and lead to a happy ending.

To house a new rat you need a spare cage. As a temporary accommodation, it does not need to be as big as the final cage, but remember that it has to provide comfort and space. You cannot predict how long the rat will be living there. All accessories: hammocks, bowls, houses, ladders etc. – have to be new or cleaned thoroughly, with no scent of other rats left on them. It is best to use water with a drop of vinegar, which helps to get rid of odor.

Put the new rat inside the cage and give it some food. Let it rest, get accustomed to a new place, and explore it. It will be surrounded by new noises and smells, so do not rush and try to introduce it to a mischief the same day. Give it some time to get used to the new situation. Remember to quarantine the newcomer, if it has not been checked by the vet yet, to be sure it does not carry any diseases or parasites. It should last at least one week.

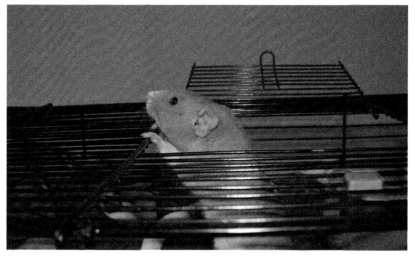

Despite some advice to keep the cages next to each other, for the rats to get accustomed to each other's smell, I recommend separating them in the very beginning. The cage with a new animal should be placed in another room, which is not filled with the scent of stationary pets. Smelling another rat, but not being able to reach it, can cause the rise of aggression, frustration, and anxiety. Moreover, a rat brought to a room filled with the smell of another individual, can become overwhelmed and scared. Keep in mind that you are also a transmitter. When attending one rat and moving to another, be sure to wash your hands. Do not use the same bowl or drinker for both rats, they also transfer the scent with them.

Keeping rats away from each other also has one more, very important benefit. The distance prevents spreading viruses and parasites, in case the newcomer turns out to be infected.

The first meeting should be conducted on neutral ground, without any scent, indicating that the territory is already occupied by another rat. It is best to use a room where neither of your critters have been present before.

STEP I - THE NEUTRAL PHASE

Before starting the neutral phase, we need to prepare ourselves and our rats.

First, take a few deep breaths and stay calm. Rats can feel our emotions, so the more nervous you are, the more tense the animals become.

Choose a neutral place for the meeting, like a bath or shower base (a whole room is too big, the space should be limited, and without a possibility to escape). A new area will be treated as no rat's territory, thus none of them will feel a need to protect it.

Preparing our pets for the first meeting, we need to take care of their scent. Rats rely heavily on smell. The detection of an unknown individual can fuel the urge to protect the territory. To prevent a fight, which can lead to serious injuries or even death, we can mask the smell of rats, to make it easier for our pets to get along. Use olive or coconut oil, and smear a tiny bit over the rats' heads, bellies, and bases of their tails. Never use any artificial substances, as rats can lick it from the fur and get sick.

To dull the alertness of a rat, you can put a few drops of natural fragrant oil on a blanket or a towel, and cover the place of meeting. Remember, that if you are doing the neutral phase in the bath or shower base, you need to put something warm at the bottom, to isolate your pets from the cold surface. The first session should last around 40 minutes to 1 hour. You can never predict how the rats will behave. Before you let them meet each other,

you must be ready for any kind of situation, including ones, that are hard to control. Prepare some tools, which will help you when your intervention is necessary. The useful set of them includes an empty tin with coins inside, to make unpleasant sounds, a sprayer with water, and a wooden or plastic ladle, long spoon or spatula, to safely separate rats, when the need occurs. It all can be really helpful when the situation gets out of hand.

Put the animals on the neutral ground and observe carefully.

If the rats are calm, and just interested in each other, it is a good sign. If you see that they are nervous, their fur is ruffled, and some stand sideways to other companions – be ready to interfere, but do not panic. It is normal for rats to try to dominate others by climbing on their backs, intensively grooming them or chasing around.

It is important to read the body language of a rat, especially when it comes to negative reactions. They can signal stress, anxiety or willingness to attack and fight. By observing a rat we can tell when the behavior is heading in the wrong direction. It also helps us with distinguishing when and how we should react, using our previously prepared tools. Squinting eyes, showing teeth, ejecting ears or putting forward whiskers are negative signs connected to the movement of the head and snout. Alarming signals associated with the body include tail wagging, sideways positioning towards the rest of the rats, climbing on another individual, just like during copulation, standing on two paws, boxing, pushing or stamping. Sound signals, which should concern you, are loud squeaking, grinding teeth, and hissing. But how can we tell when it is a proper time for us to react?

Remember, it is better safe than sorry. When the signals are strong and burdensome for the bothered rat, it is time to react, in order to avoid a fight. First, let's use what we always have with us – our voice and hands. When the rat is getting aggressive towards another individual, and you want to correct the behavior, make some unpleasant noise for a critter to distract it and cool down the enthusiasm for a scuffle. Make a loud *"sheesh"* sound - it should be irritating for the animal. Then add the name of your pet in a confident voice. Rats are very fast learners, and they can memorize when you refer to them, just like dogs, by repetition. They also react to the modulation of the voice. Your action will hopefully temper the recent attitude of the attacker. After a while it can try to repeat the same behavior. In such a case you have to follow the process once again, until it loses the interest in assaulting another rat. If your voice does not work – use your hands and clap. Loud and sudden sounds should startle the rat and make it freeze for some time. If your claps and voice signals are still not enough – it is time to use our previously prepared tools.

Standing on hind legs, with lifted head, signalizes willingness to attack. In such a situation - be ready to use the can. Shake it to produce an unpleasant sound. It is far worse for rats than our clapping or sheeshing, and should discourage the rat from attacking. If, despite the warning, our pet decides to push forward – separate it from another individual by using the ladle or spatula, gently and slowly. Just put the tool between two animals, and calmly and steadily increase the distance between them, by pushing the aggressor away. Sudden,

quick movements of the ladle or spatula can only make the rat more determined to harm its opponent.

Never use your bare hand to separate fighting rats! You may regret it after a stressed animal bites you instead of its rival. As a last resort you can use a thick glove, nonetheless the animal will probably release its aggression on your fingers, or can even jump to your wrists or upper, not protected parts of your arm.

Aside from body movement, pay attention to the sounds. The submissive rat can make quiet squeaking noise, but it is acceptable until you hear loud, panicked peeps. Then it is time to interfere. First with the can. If no results – push away the attacker with the spoon or spatula, just as described above.

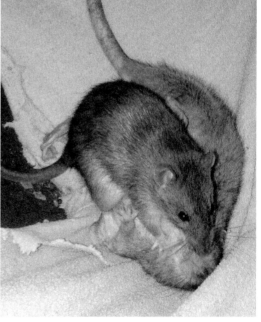

Positive reactions, forecasting a quick bonding, include licking and sniffing another rat, grooming, snuggling or just lying next to each other, or even in a distance, but in general this position indicates relaxation and calmness. When you see that rats feel comfortable in the group, they do not try to fight but instead are resting together, cuddling or just minding their own business – you can move to the next phase.

STEP TWO – THE PICKLING

This is a phase I like to call the pickling, because just like cucumbers squeezed inside a jar, rats are doomed to their own company. Limited space forces animals to exist close to each other, nowhere to run or hide. Though it may sound cruel, it really helps with creating a bond between the whole group.

For this phase you need a cage, big enough for all the rats to move around freely, but at the same time with restricted space, so they are forced to interact with each other. The cage has to be appropriately prepared. It is essential for the airflow to be suitable. High concentration of rats in a limited area means a lot of ammonia fumes.

If the cage is not new – you have to clean it thoroughly. You can add a little bit of vinegar to neutralize the scent of previous tenants. Put some pellets on the bottom – do not let your rats stand in their own pee – you cannot predict for how long they have to stay there. Remember also to add a drinker and food – but do not put it in one place, scatter some tasty treats all around the cage. When looking for them, rats have to move around other members of the group instead of sitting in one corner. Do not put any houses, hammocks or boxes, places for rats to hide, inside. Leave rats in such an environment and observe their behavior.

A little scuffle is acceptable, unless you see a negative behavior leading to a fight, described before. You can also use your tools during this phase, especially a can, as it can be hard to reach a rat with a ladle in

a closed cage. When the blood appears, you have to go back to the neutral phase and patiently try again.

This phase should last at least one day. If no aggressive behavior occurs, and your rats seem to feel comfortable in each other's company, you can start preparations for the next step. If you are not sure that all individuals became accepted in the group, you can prolong this period even up to three days. Just remember to keep the cage clean, and supply your critters with more tasty treats.

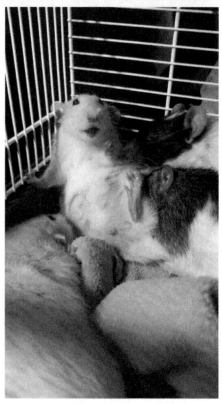

PHASE THREE – A COMMON HOUSE

When your rats have finally learned to peacefully coexist, it is time to put them in a target cage. Do not require them to love each other, the most important aspect is for them to not show any signs of aggression, and be at least neutral to all companions. It is best to limit the space in the cage, for example by blocking upper levels. Let your pets get used to their final home bit by bit. Fill the bottom with substrate, add drinkers and few sources of food. The cage should be emptied of any accessories, hammocks, homes, toys - they can become the apple of discord. You can gradually add them day by day, if the situation in the group is stable. During this phase do not let your rats out of the cage yet for a few more days. Let them settle down and learn the rules of living in a new group.

PHASE FOUR - AN OUTSIDE PLAYGROUND

First time out of the cage for the whole group should be conducted in a limited space. It helps with the observation of the rats, as well and prevents them from dispersing and hiding in every corner. There are some basic rules you have to follow in order to keep your pets safe. Before opening the cage, remember about securing the area. Close all the doors and windows – you will be surprised how high a rat can climb! Block gaps behind the shelves, under the wardrobe or to any space, where your pet can get stuck. Secure all food store areas, trash bins, wires, and power sockets. Move all the plants your rats can have access to – many house plants are toxic. Do not leave your rodents with other pets in one room. Be sure that a cat or dog is not able to open the door, or get inside in any other way. You should keep an eye on rats during the whole time they are outside the cage.

The behavior of some rats can change outside the safe and known area of the cage. New territory can increase the level of anxiety, stress or aggression. That is why rats should be introduced to being outside the cage gradually. Start with a few sessions, lasting around fifteen minutes. Remember to enrich the space with toys, hammocks, and digging boxes. This should be an active time for your pets. Be together with your pets for the whole time. In case of negative behavior, use tips

described above to suppress it. Each day leave the cage open for a longer period of time.

After a few tries, with no worrying signals, you can increase the space for your rats to explore. Keep in mind that these little critters are very curious, and can try to find a way out of the intended area, or try to squeeze through very small holes, so supervision is very important. Additionally, time with your rats creates a bond between you and them. This is your time together, to

play, cuddle, and relax in each others' company. It should last at least one, two hours per day.

The connection between a human and a rat is as important as a bond created between the members of the mischief. Some animals tend to show aggression or fear towards people, mostly due to stress or trauma. Such behavior must be corrected. As an owner and a keeper, we must be able to safely touch our critter, examine or pick it up.

First days in a new home can be very stressful for rats – new place, new smells and sounds, it all can discourage these critters from any activity. They will rather stay hidden in some safe place. We should not force them to come out, do not pet them, or pick them up if they show any signs of fear or nervousness. Let them slowly get used to the new situation. Surely, our goal is to socialize them, but imposing ourselves

can only worsen the situation. There are few ways to safely speed up this bonding process.

- Take a shirt, blouse, or any piece of clothing, wear it for the whole day, and instead of throwing it into the washing machine, put it inside the rats' cage. It will help the critters with getting used to your smell.

- Take something delicious, with an intense smell – it can be a little piece of boiled fish (watch out for the bones!) or a good quality meat, an egg or broccoli. First, put it in front of you. It will encourage the rat to come closer, lured by the scent. Reduce the distance between the treat and you, eventually keep it in your hand, and wait for the animal to grab it from you.

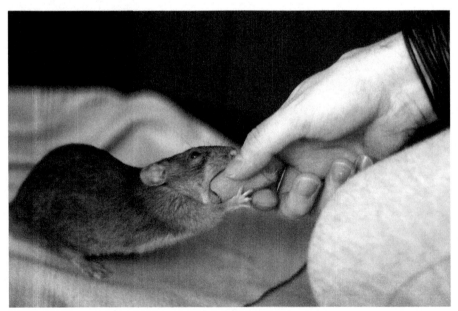

- When your rat is more familiar with your scent, and there is no risk of being bitten, you can try to encourage it to lick your hand. Blend some fruits, mix them with honey or peanut butter, add some water, and smear the *cocktail* on your fingertips. Rats will associate your fingers with something tasty and will be less scared of your touch.

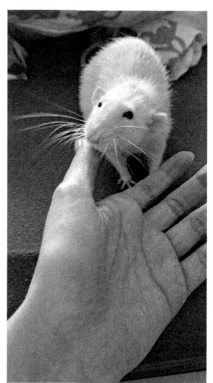

- Decide where the cage should be placed – in the kitchen, living room or the hall – and expose the animal to all kinds of sounds which can surprise it, bit by bit. For Example, in the kitchen a dropped pot can make a lot of noise. Let's try to prepare our rodents for such a sudden and loud sound, by softly hitting the pot, making it generate less scary sounds. Turn on the TV in the living room, gradually increasing the volume. Let the dog bark in the same room

where the cage is placed. Keep in mind, that it is only natural for rats to run and hide, when they hear any kind of suspicious sound, so these procedures will not make them sit calmly in a noisy environment, but can reduce the stress, and help them feel safer in sudden, loud situations.

- Read a book aloud in the presence of the rat to make it more used to your voice.

- When the rat is more familiar with your scent, you can move to getting it used to being picked up. Take something tasty between your thumb and a pointing finger. Hold it, and let the animal start the consumption. Gently pat the critter with your finger, then two – three fingers, and finally your whole hand. If the rodent is calm – try to slowly pick it up. If it starts to feel nervous – slow

down and go back to patting with your fingers. There is no need to rush.

FEAR AND AGGRESSION

When adopting rats from foster homes or rescue societies, we can never be sure about their past, how they were treated, what conditions they used to live in. Some animals can behave aggressively or be terrified in an unknown environment, and avoid any contact with humans. Such individuals need time and special treatment to help them accommodate, and enjoy their life in a new home.

Working with problematic rats – both aggressive and skittish – looks quite similar, as very often the aggression is caused by fear. First of all, you have to be patient, as getting rid of unwanted behavior can last a few weeks or even months.
Follow the steps described above. Observe the behavior. A frightened rat will hide or freeze while hearing your voice or smelling you. Such an individual needs more time to feel safe and confident in the new environment. When the animal is shy and skittish, try to feed it from your hand as often as possible. Choose a special treat that will be available for your pet only during this process. After several times, try to touch it – only with the palm of your finger - while the rat is occupied with eating. If the animal still retreats when your hand approaches it, more time is needed. Be patient and consistently encourage your critter to not be scared of your hand. When the time comes and the rat allows you to touch it – stroke it calmly.

Just remember to pet parallelly to the animal's body. Do not try to tickle your critter or make any sudden movements. You also have to remember that some rats can be more timid than others, and will never be very social towards humans. Not all of them like to be picked up or touched. You should not treat such behavior as something negative, as simply different rats have different personalities, just like people. We have to accept it. But there is one demeanor which we cannot turn a blind eye to - biting. This behavior must be rooted out, and below you will find some hints on how to do it.

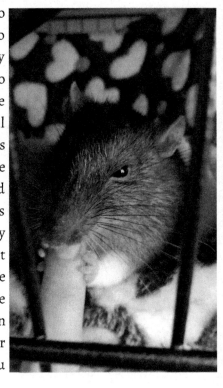

As already mentioned before, fear is one of the most common factors leading to aggressive behavior in rats. Next in line is sex. Male rats are more likely to exhibit such demeanor. In most groups a male individual gains the status of an alpha, the leader of the mischief. Agressive attitude is therefore fueled by the willingness to dominate others, sometimes including humans, and additionaly – by testosterone, a sex male hormone produced in testicles. That is why, after spotting an offensive behavior in males, the first step should be neutering. Benefits are in both, physical and mental spheres. As you should already know by now, breeding rats should be performed only by the professionals, so additionally, such a procedure brings an ease to a male animal, unable to follow its instinct to reproduce. It also prevents many health issues from developing. Just remember that a time is needed for a testosterone level to decline. Usually it takes around two weeks, so do not expect the behavior to improve immediately.

Some people are afraid that neutering a rat makes it lazy and sluggish. It is true that animal's behavior can change after this procedure, but mostly in a positive way. Neutered males are calmer, easier to handle and socialize. Additionally, they stop marking their territory with urine.

Dealing with an aggressive individual can be quite troublesome and time consuming. As already mentioned before, rats can feel your emotions, and fear is one of them. Sensing your insecurity, they are more likely to attack, so always try to stay calm in the presence of an aggressive critter. Signals foretelling an attack look the same as the ones already described above. Rats do not have a different set of them for humans. The procedure of timing an aggressive individual also looks similar to socializing a timid rat, but it can be more dangerous, so always remember about your safety.

Leave the troublesome pet for the first day alone in the cage. Give it tasty treats to make the stressful change of the surroundings more pleasant. Keep the cage in the room where you spend most of your time, to expose the animal to your smell, voice, and everyday-life sounds. Next, try to give the rat a treat, but not through the bars. Open the gate carefully and not when the animal is right behind it. If it is too close, wait for the rat to be in a safe distance. Put something tasty, like dried mealworm, piece of avocado or a nut, inside the cage, withdraw your hand and wait. Do not try to hand feed the critter yet! After a few tries, when the animal is not trying to attack you, keep your hand behind the treat, but always in a safe distance. Be ready to withdraw it if needed. This procedure helps the pet associate your fingers with a pleasant experience, a tasty food instead of an easy target for biting.

Unfortunately, a calm behavior in the cage does not equal a calm rat in the open, so the procedure of socializing an aggressive individual also has to take place outside the bars. The area for a rat to use should be smaller than normally advised, just like in the case of joining a mischief. Be sure it is safe – it will be extremely hard to catch a terrified, biting rat once it escapes! Enrich the place with toys – digging boxes, balls and olfactory mats filled with tasty treats. This will help with the stress relief, and encourage the animal to focus more on the surroundings, rather than yourself. Do not put any houses or boxes, in which the rat can hide, in the area. It can get inside and stay there for a long time, which is not the point of this process. Similarly, the cage, a well known environment, full of shelter spots, cannot be situated anywhere inside the socializing place.

Do not try to pick up an aggressive or scared rat, even when wearing thick gloves. Believe me, most of them cannot protect you from rats' teeth. Use a rodent carrier to transport the animal. Lure it inside with a tasty treat and safely move it to the destined place in the container.

Rat attacks can cause serious injuries to the human body, that is why you always have to stay alert. During the time of socializing with your pet, also abide by some rules. Firstly, protect your body. Dress up properly – choose thick pants or jeans, put two or even three pairs of socks on, cover your arms with sleeves, and try to keep your hands away from rodents' teeth.

Do not try to touch an aggressive rat. Keep the can and ladle, or wooden spoon, mentioned in the previous chapter about socializing rats, with you. Use a can to make an unpleasant sound, when the rat is willing to attack you. Look for already described signals - side body positioning, standing on hind legs, ruffled fur, hissing. If the critter comes too close to your body, do not move, use your voice to discourage the animal from striking. *Sheesh* and say loud and confident – no. As a last resort use a ladle to push the animal further from you, do it gently. Never do it with your bare hands!

If the problematic individual is not interested in you - do not try to interact with it. Just let it roam freely and monitor the situation. Let the animal get used to your presence. It must learn that it does not mean any danger.

Patience and regularity are the key to success. Such time outside the cage with your pet has to be organized two, three times a day, each day, and last about fifteen, twenty minutes. Postpone your vacation or trips if you have to tame an aggressive rat. A break in the process, even for one day, can cause a recession in the behavior. Gradually, you can prolong the time you spend with the rat. It must learn that you mean no harm, and your presence does not require an offensive attitude. Take some tasty snacks with you. If the rat does not show any signs of aggression – reward it. If any disturbing behavior occurs, *sheesh* or use the can to cut it short. When the time comes, and you will be able to touch your troublesome pet without your fingers being bitten, do not try to tickle it or take it on hand yet. Step after step, slowly pet it with one, two and three fingers. After one, two days use your whole hand, and finally try to pick up the animal. If you notice any worrying

signals – go back to previous steps, and patiently repeat the cycle. Believe me, it is worth your while, and you will be amazed how rat's behavior can change over a month with your proper guidance.

If the rat is not aggressive toward other members of the mischief, they can join you during the process of socialization. When there is already a bond between the animals, they make the procedure easier and diminish the occurrence of offensive behavior. But always keep in mind that the attitude toward another rat can change rapidly in stressful situations, and the aggressive individual can start to attack other members of the group.

Despite some advice in many sources, to try to dominate your aggressive rat by placing it on its back, and holding it like this until it calms down, I strongly advise against such a method. Even if you are desperate. It works when animals establish

hierarchy in their own group, and an alpha wants to demonstrate its strength. But when done by people, it only increases the level of aggression and stress your rat feels, while forced to stay in such a position. Moreover, the animal can perceive you as an enemy after such an incident. Even if it calms down, being on its back, it will probably start furiously biting your hand the moment you loosen your grip. Such tries of desperate dominance will only make it harder to create a bond with your rat, and cam trigger more attacks.

Though you should never breed rats if you are not a professional breeder, it can happen that a pregnant female will one day come to your house. It is essential to know how to take care of a future mummy and her babies.

Breeding rats on your own is very irresponsible, and should not be performed. Not knowing the past of an animal, its gene pool and health issues it can carry along, can result in the birth of individuals struggling with many illnesses. Moreover, there are many rats waiting for their forever homes in shelters, foster care and charities, so you should not contribute to the increase of critters in need.

Female rats have an estrus period every 5-8 days and it lasts approximately 6-8 days. If fertilization occurs, the average gestation time lasts around 22 days. It is possible to notice changes in a female's body after two weeks. She gains weight and her belly grows. During the first half of the pregnancy the food portion should be increased by 1/3 of daily amount. Especially products rich in protein, being the building material for the body of the future babies, are important. The female should also be given proper materials, like tissue paper or soft cloth, as soon she will start to feel the need to build a nest. Some moms-to-be get nervous around other rats, so it is safer to separate them from other members of the group. Be sure to have another cage prepared for the pregnant female, with proper facilities - calm, dark hiding place to build a nest in, and without any stairs, ladders or floors – for the safety of future pups.

The more advanced the pregnancy is, the more peace, rest and of course food is needed by the female. The daily dose should be doubled. She should not be taken on hand if not really necessary during this time. Some females get very sensitive during pregnancy and do not like to be touched at all. Even docile and friendly ones can become aggressive and bite, so they should not be bothered by us.

If a pregnant female rat is stressed for a long time or the conditions of living are not favorable for having babies at the moment, she is able to absorb the embryo to save the body reserves, and wait for a more proper time to give birth.

LABOR

Just before the labor, a female rat hides in the previously built nest. She should be left alone, not bothered or touched at all during this moment. She will soon feel painful contractions. The labor usually lasts up to a few hours.

Female rat can give birth to twenty pups in one litter – it depends on her condition, age, food quality, and many other factors. Very young females have smaller litters. There is also a higher chance that they will give birth to dead pups, or will not manage to raise all of them.

When the babies are born, either head or bottom first, mother licks each one of them, not only to clean the body, but also to stimulate the blood circulation system, as well as to learn the smell. This is also a moment when a bond between a baby and the mom is being created. Often females eat fetal membranes and placenta to retrieve nutrients that they contain, to recover faster after the birthing process.

Though it happens rarely, rat mothers sometimes eat their own babies after labor. There are many reasons for such a behavior, but mainly it is caused by stress, scarcity of food, illness, injury or death of a pup. Hormonal changes, mental issues, like postpartum depression, can also lead to such events. That is why it is so important to ensure proper conditions for a pregnant rat, and provide it with peace during pregnancy and labor.

Under any circumstances do not touch or move the nest for at least four days from the birth. The one exception is the risk of death of the litter. Do not clean the area. You can remove food scraps,  poops or other filth near the babies, but do not touch the nest. The mother will keep it clean enough. For tidying the whole cage you have to wait at least two weeks. If the necessity occurs for you to touch the nest or the baby, for example when a dangerous object comes too close to pups, or they get stuck or tangled in the nest, find a moment when the female is occupied with food, or at least is not in the den – not to stress her. Also, you have to be aware that the disturbance of the smell, caused by your touch, can make a mother abandon her newborn babies, although this happens rather rarely.

The younger the pups, the shorter the time they can be left without their mom, giving them food and warmth. Nonetheless, you also have to remember that a fresh mommy needs a little break, and should have an opportunity to spend a moment away from the litter. Let her out of a cage daily for a short amount of time. In the meantime, you can also join the female with other group members. Just remember about closing the cage when the mom is out, for the pups' safety. Sometimes the mother looks for a better hiding place for her litter, and can start carrying out baby rats from their nest. She can put them in many unexpected places – under the pillows, into slippers, inside the drawer with underwear. Good luck finding the little ones then! They can be unconsciously crushed, stepped on, attacked by another pet or just die from starvation or hypothermia, unattended by their mother.

Some female rats are so obsessed with maternity that they can steal other mum's pups, hide them in their own nest, and guard them from other individuals, even their biological mother. It can be quite dangerous, not only for the babies, but also for the thief-mom, as she can take so many little rats that her organism can get exhausted by trying to take care of all of them.
On the other hand, such behavior can have a very positive aspect. A litter abandoned by one mother can be adopted by another, and raised as her own. Sometimes when females have litter at a similar time, they raise the pups together.

RAT PUPS

Rat pups are born blind and deaf. They are often called pinkies, due to the color of their hairless bodies. They measure less than 1,5 inch, and weigh around seven grams. For now, their only goal in life is to suck a nipple and drink their mother's milk. It contains four and a half times more fat and over three times more protein than cow's milk. It has to supply fast developing organs and tissues. Pinkies have to triple their weight during the first ten days. Many changes occur in their small bodies, starting from the very beginning. Pups' ears begin to develop by day three. Soon after, toes and fingers separate from each other. At the end of first week pinkies are more active, and already covered in peach fuzz hair. Sex can be determined now, though it is better to wait until pups are around two weeks old, as picking them up at such a young age can stress them. We can also unintentionally harm their fragile bodies.

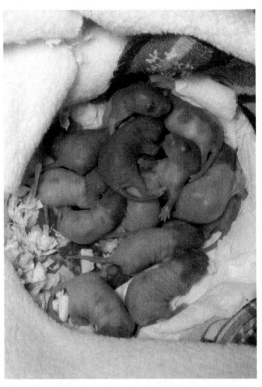

The distance between the pup's anus and genitals can tell us the sex of a rat. In males it is almost twice as long as in female's.

After ten days pups' ears separate from the head, though they are still deaf. Babies begin to crawl, but they need a few more days to be able to walk. Later they explore their surroundings carefully, examining all around them with the sense of touch. Their mother patiently brings them back to the nest if they wander too far. Pups' movements can be quite uncoordinated, due to their still developing nervous system. Their incisors begin to appear during the second week of their lives, and soon after their eyes and ear canals open. They see and hear now.

The third week is crucial for the litter. It is high time to start socializing. We can now slowly try to take baby rats on hand and touch them. During the playtime

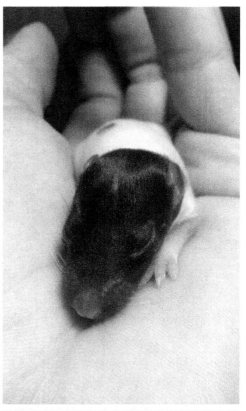

remember about safety, as pups can move quite fast now. The control over their own bodies increases greatly, and they become very active. It is a time for more play, less sleep, as well as new experiences and tastes. Baby rats start to sample food given to their mother, so the amount of vegetables, fruits and grains should be slightly increased. After eighteen days from the birth, pups can run, climb, jump, and are ready to inhabit a bigger cage with more area to play around. They start to show different behavior, some are more shy, some outgoing, confident and curious.

Week four is the last one for the whole family to spend together. All babies are weaned now, though

occasionally some individuals can be nursed a little longer. They learn from their mom what kind of food is safe to consume. You may notice that when given a treat, momma rat quickly becomes swarmed by her babies, wanting to try what she has just nibbled. Be sure to give the female a tasty meal away from her babies from time to time. A dinner in peace will be much appreciated.

At the age of five weeks males must be separated from their mother and sisters, as pups will soon become sexualy mature. The rest of the family can be kept together, and be carefully joined with the rest of the group.

THE ABANDONMENT OF THE YOUNG

Sometimes it happens that a mother abandons her pups after labor and does not want to feed them or care for them. It can be caused by a female's young age, stress, health problems, and many other factors. By evaluating her present situation, mamma rat can decide that having offspring at this time can endanger her life, or predict that the litter will not manage to survive. There are three solutions to this kind of situation – finding a foster mother, raising the pups on your own, or euthanasia. Though the last choice seems quite cruel, in some cases this is the best for pups, especially when we cannot find a foster mom. Raising the pups is very challenging. Even when closely following the rules, it is very easy to harm a baby. If you are not one hundred percent sure that you have time and full determination to pick up this challenge – do not experiment on pinkies. Do not try and just check if you can manage, and do not sentence them to die slowly from malnutrition, hypothermia or choking. Take into consideration that they need frequent feeding even during a night, almost 24/7 care.

FOSTER MOTHER

Mother rats are mostly willing to adopt orphaned babies, best if they are at a similar level of development of their own litter. Though it seems hard to find such a foster mom, it is worth trying, as this method gives the biggest chance of survival for the orphaned pups.

Look for foster moms in local rodent charities, ask on social media, search on rat lovers groups.

Before placing orphaned rat pups in the nest, get the foster mother out of it. Put babies inside, and let the scent of the nest and other pinkies transfer to them. Carefully observe the female's behavior after releasing her near the den. If she is not interested in new pups and does not take care of them, you can move the whole family to a smaller cage. It can help with creating a bond between all members, just like in case of introducing a new rat to the mischief. Give the female some time, there is a high chance that she will accept the babies and raise them as her own.

THE LAST RESORT

The most challenging, but sometimes the only available method of helping abandoned pups, is to raise them yourself. It is a very hard and time consuming enterprise. The younger the babies, the smaller the chance for them to survive without their mom.

The abandoned babies must be supplied with a safe and warm environment, without any object that can hurt them. If you do not have a proper, safe cage, a cardboard box can be useful during the first weeks, until 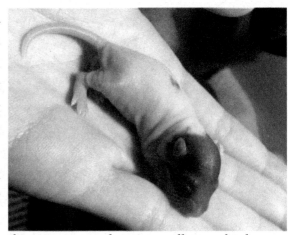 the pups' eyes are still shut. Be sure that its walls are high enough. If a mama rat managed to make a nest – use it. If not – you are responsible for providing a safe den for the pinkies. Use soft and smooth material – tissue paper, cloth or fleece (fabric without dangerous, loose threads like from knitted jumpers, and without buttons or metal elements) and form a donut. Remember that baby rats are not able to maintain their body temperature. They need a source of warmth to survive. Normally, it is the mother's body that keeps them warm. The best idea is to have a permanent source of warmth available for pinkies, like a heating pad or heating light bulb. You can also use a hot water bottle, but be sure to check the temperature regularly, and reheat it when necessary. Remember to always leave a space in the box where pups can crawl to, when they feel too hot, without any source of warmth. Be careful with light bulbs and pads, as they can get very hot and burn or even kill fragile pups! Secure them properly.

Regardless of the source of warmth, you must constantly monitor the temperature in the box. To be sure that it is proper, keep a weather thermometer next to the babies. It should point around 37,5 – 38,5 °C (99,5 101,5 °F), to be sure that babies are not cold. Too high or low temperatures can result in pups' death. Little rats can easily develop pneumonia. If you hear strange, clicking noise while the baby is breathing, call your vet immediately. Quick reaction can save their lives.

FOOD

For such fragile and helpless creatures proper feeding determines the chances of survival. Caring about rats' hygiene and temperature may not seem too problematic, but feeding them is another story. Baby rats need to eat every 2-4 hours, even during the night. If you are not able to maintain a routine, they will suffer from the lack of nutrients or body poisoning.

Firstly, be sure that you have proper food for the babies. You need to find the formula which is most similar to mother's milk, which contains 13% of fat, 9,7% protein, and 3,2% lactose. Cow milk is not suitable as it does not have the right balance of nutrients for rats, and does not support adequate growth of their organism. Additionally, it can make pups sick, and even kill them. As a last resort you can feed them fresh goat milk, home-made formulas (made from water, sugar or glucose, and yolk), but the safest and most adequate will be powdered formulas which you can get at pet stores or at the veterinary clinics. It is not easy to get a formula for rats, but the one for kittens, dog puppies or even human infants is also suitable. In fact, these last ones can be the best choice, as the percentage of protein and fat matches closely that of a rat's milk.

The powder formula has to be dissolved in water. It is recommended to use a more dilute mixture during the first week of life – for the first feeding, prepare a formula which contains 4 parts of water and 1 part of powder. During next feedings, gradually increase the amount of powder, to finally reach 2 parts of water to 1 part of powder. Remember, it is better for the formula to be too diluted than too thick! Bad proportions can lead to choking and death of the baby.

Be sure that the food has a proper temperature, it cannot be too cold or too hot – just pleasantly warm, like the body temperature. While feeding more babies at the same time, be sure that the formula stays warm until the last one of them. Heat it during feeding time. Make fresh formula each time you do the feeding, it easily goes bad.

To feed the babies you need 1 ml syringe – of course without a needle! - and dropper. In some pet shops or vet clinics you can get rubber endings to apply to a syringe, which will imitate the mother's nipple, and make it easier for the baby to suckle. Do not get demotivated when the baby is not willing to eat from such a tool at first. The

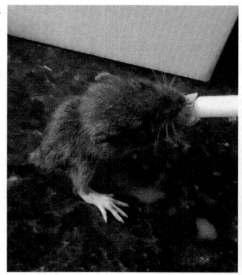

animal also needs some time to get used to this method of feeding.

Baby rat should eat around 5% of its weight per one meal - so a gram scale will be an essential purchase. To begin with, warm your hands before picking up the rat, you can either warm them in hot water or by rubbing them. Little rats are very sensitive to temperature changes.

To avoid the risk of choking, place the baby in the right position – its body should be set vertically, while the snout horizontally. It can take around 5 minutes to feed one baby, so feeding the whole litter can be time-consuming. Just remember not to hurry and be very gentle. Never try to put the milk directly into the baby's mouth. Put the dropper in front of a rat and wait until it suckles. Otherwise it can inhale the milk (via mouth and nose – pinkies cannot sneeze yet, so be sure that their nose is always dry!). Pressing the syringe plunger too fast can lead to choking, and eventually death. Bubbles coming out of the nose is a sign that the baby is literally drowning, as the formula floods its lungs.

After feeding the pinkies, the formula in their bellies is visible via thin skin. It is a good practice to check it for bubbles of gas, which can be very painful for the baby. The easiest way to get rid of them is to gently massage the belly sides, just under the ribs, with your fingers. Alway keep the baby warm. Otherwise it will not be able to digest the food.

Feeding frequency depends on the age of a baby:

- 1 week – every 1-2,5 hour, even during the night, so there should be 6-7 feedings.
- 2 weeks – every 3-4 hours, also during the night, 5-6 feeding.
- 3 weeks – every 4-5 hours, we can try to stop feeding the babies during the night. First feeding should take place early in the morning, the last one just before going to bed.
- 4 weeks – babies should start to chew on more solid food. Boiled rice or groats can be added to their diet.
- 5 weeks - baby rats should have solid food, fruits and vegetables available.
- 6-7 weeks – we can stop feeding the babies with the formula, they should now switch to solid food, and have a diet like adult ones.

HYGIENE

Mother rats take care of pups' hygiene, as the babies are not able to control their own bodies yet. When a female is gone, it is you who needs to replace her. It is essential to stimulate the baby, by rubbing around their genitals and anus, in order to help it defecate. You can gently pick up a pinkie and place it on an open hand. Use a little piece of tissue or a cotton ball, dip it in warm water, and brush across the genitals and anus. By imitating mother's licking, you help the baby to empty the bladder and bowels. Little rats should pee after every feeding, and poop after at least every third. Do not be surprised by the different color of the excrements, it can be yellow or brown. It is also softer than an adult's dung. It changes and hardens once the rat switches to solid food. Do not hold a baby too long in your hand, and always make sure that its body is entirely dry, before returning it to the nest.

Helping babies with defecation is essential during at least the first two weeks. Keep in mind that ignoring this procedure leads to the death of the pinkies. It is caused by the toxic poisoning of the body from their own waste.

Diarrhea occurs quite often while feeding small rodents, and can be very problematic. It can be caused by overfeeding, changing the formula or – what is more dangerous – various bacteria or parasites. If you see that the poo is liquid, there is no time to wait, contact your vet immediately. Baby rats can dehydrate very quickly. Eventually, it leads to death.

Check the level of hydration by gently lifting the skin on the animal's back. It should quickly return and wrap the body. If the skin stays loose, and it takes time for it to come back to its proper shape, it means that the animal is dehydrated.

OLD AGE

The average domestic rat's life lasts for 2 - 3 years. The health of these animals can rapidly deteriorate after entering the senior age. Elder rats should be treated differently than young ones, as their needs change with their age.

After your critters turn two years old, be prepared for regular vet checks. It is really important to diagnose any health problems as soon as possible. It gives older rats the best chance of recovery. Delaying any surgeries decreases the probability for the animal to wake up from anesthesia, and for quick recovery. Remember about the dental checks. Some older rats can have

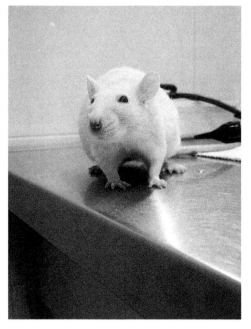

problems with chewing tough food, what leads to problems with incisors.

Sometimes the adjustment of the cage is essential, as the age brings blindness and impairment of movement for most of the rats. At some point your rats will no longer be agile enough to climb every ladder or to jump from one platform to another. The space between them should be decreased, to minimize the chance of falling. Add more hammocks beneath shelves in the cage, to assure soft landing in case of slipping. The fall from the top of the cage can cause serious health problems. You can put a pillow at the bottom. It will, of course, absorb all smelly liquids, but it is better to wash it often than risk a broken paw.

Be sure that the source of

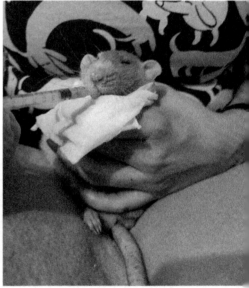

food and water is always accessible for your pets. It is best to place them at the bottom of the cage now.

If you notice that younger rats bother your elders - separate them. Some animals tend to bully weaker individuals, or take all the food for themselves. If such behavior does not occur, it is better for your elder pets to have company. Often younger rats help their old companions clean themselves or navigate the surroundings.

Over time rats lose their flexibility and mobility, thus caring for their coat gets harder for them. Some can have problems with urinary incontinence, leading to skin irritation and inflammation. In such cases you have to help your friend with their hygiene. Check their bum and belly, wipe it dry if needed. If the skin condition is getting worse, contact your vet.

Some rats' lives end peacefully, they leave us during their sleep. Unfortunately, in most cases it is our responsibility to choose the proper moment. Many critters' owners ask, when is this right time. One vet once told me, the right time for any animal to be euthanized is when it is no longer able to take care of basic needs on its own: to move (of course in some cases the wheelchair helps, but not necessarily with rats), feed, or defecate, and there is no chance for improvement. Obviously, also when the animal feels constant pain, and there is no way to cure it. Such conditions deteriorate the level of comfort of living. It is better to let go than condemn our beloved pet to feel the pain, without the possibility to enjoy life.

RATS IN DIFFERENT CULTURES

Studying rats in culture, folklore and religion, a division in the approach to these critters can be observed, depending on the geographical aspect. The East seems to perceive them in a less negative way than the western regions. It is mainly influenced by the religious sphere and beliefs of strong connection between animals and gods. Respect for every living creature, being a part of one big universe, and unity with nature, seems to be the core features of eastern spirituality.

In Hinduism many gods are represented by certain animals. This fact not only emphasizes the sacredness of every life, but also its equality. Moreover, the belief of reincarnation vividly shows that animals are believed to have souls - deeds committed in your present life impacts your next ones. A life without love, respect, and kindness leads to the degradation of the soul, which eventually reincarnates into pig, spider, lizard or any animal of lower level of dignity. Stealing food can result in being reborn as a rat! That is why all living creatures are sacred, and it is forbidden to hurt them, as they could once be humans in their past life. Hindus also believe that feeding animals is their duty to Mother Nature. That is why in Deshnok town in India, people feed around twenty thousand rats in the

temple of Karni Mata. They bring milk, grain, fruits and coconut shells, as a part of worshiping these critters. Here rats are called little children, and are under firm protection. It is strictly forbidden to hurt them, not to mention killing. If even by an accident a life is taken from the animal, the culprit is required to bring a gold or silver statue of a creature, as a compensation. Rats owe this piece of heaven to a woman sage warrior born in the VIX century, Karni Mata, and the legend connected to her life. According to the beliefs, after the loss of her step son, she asked Yama, a god of death, to bring the child back. The deity gave the boy back in the form of a rat, and promised that all descendants of Karni Mata will be reincarnated as these animals.

Thanks to this godly interference little rodents gained the

status of sacred creatures. Seeing a white rat in Karni Mata Temple means luck. You can enter the building only barefoot, having a chance of being blessed by a rat touching your feet.

In Hindu mythology a rat, or a mouse, is also depicted as a vehicle of Ganesha, the god of prosperity and wisdom. Though it may seem strange, seeing an elephant headed deity riding a tiny rodent, there is a story, explaining this phenomenon. Rat was once a god, called Krauncha. One day he insulted a sage, who turned him into a giant rodent. The deity became unable to control its huge body, and destroyed all on its way, including a place where Ganesha was resting. To stop the devastation, the god of prosperity decided to catch the beast, and shrink it. As a punishment, Krauncha asked to be the god's mount. But he was so small now, that it was impossible.

Finally, Ganesha reduced his weight, and was able to ride the rodent. There is also a symbolic meaning behind this duo. As a rat represents a restless mind, Ganesha is able to restrain it with his wisdom and calmness. Both of them also symbolize intelligence and ability to overcome differnet obstacles.

Similar to Hinduism, Buddhism also treats

animals as creatures demanding respect and fair treatment. The idea of reincarnation, and vegetarianism are the main foundations of this religion. As a consequence of eating meat, one can be reborn as a demon, feeding only on flesh. Buddha taught that no living creature must be harmed, even a troublesome one like a rat. He also established a Chinese Zodiac with the help of different animals. There are many versions of this legend, but one says that before leaving the Earth, Buddha wanted to say goodbye to all creatures. He sent invitations for the last meeting, and organized the Great Race. Twelve creatures responded and took part in the event. One stage included crossing a vast river. Rat was running along the cat, when they stopped at the bank. When the ox joined them, the rodent suggested taking advantage of the strong animal, and crossed the river on its back. But when they were just about to reach the other side, the rat pushed the cat into the water, and jumped out of the ox's head to finish the race first. As a winner, he became the first animal in the Chinese Zodiac. Later came the ox, tiger, rabbit, dragon, snake, horse, goat, monkey, rooster, dog, and pig, establishing the order of the zodiac cycle. Thanks to its action, the rat not only won the race, but also became a symbol of resourcefulness and cleverness, though some perceive it also as sly and cunning.

People born in the year of the rat are believed to be optimistic, hardworking and energetic, though they can also be very stubborn and jealous.

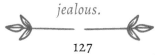

For Chinese people, rats are a symbol of wealth and surplus. Having these rodents at home meant that there was plenty of food inside. Some believe that dreaming about a rat foretells riches, good harvest for farmers, and offsprings for married couples, as these rodents also signify fertility.

Koreans treat twelve zodiac animals as guardian spirits, and rat is believed to have great wisdom. In the myth about the Creation of the Universe, a rat or mouse, which in the past were often not distinguished, leads the God of Creation to the source of water in the mountains. It also reveals to him the secret of fire, by hitting iron with a rock.

In Japan the approach to rats is similar to other eastern countries. They bring good fortune. A god of wealth, luck and grain – Daikokuten, is often accompanied by a rat, which, due to the legend, saved the deity's life. Other gods grew jealous of Daikokuten's popularity among the devotees, and decided to get rid of the contestant. A god of death sent a cunning demon, Shiro, on this mission. A rat, spotting the approaching danger, ran to the garden and brough Daikokuten a branch of holly to

drive the enemy away. The plant was believed to have magical powers. Until today Daikokuten is one of the most popular and worshiped gods, pictured with his rat friend.

Aside from being identified with wealth and luck, rats

gained yet another form in Japanese folklore, a form of a warning. Tesso, an Iron Claw Rat, is a demon that haunts those who break promises. Originally, he was a monk, called Raigo, who helped the emperor welcome his son, by eager prayers. The ruler was so overjoyed with his offspring, that he pledged to build a monastery for the monk. But not everybody liked the idea, and soon the emperor was bribed by rival monks to stop his project. Raigo became furious and disappointed, and went on a hunger strike, as there was nothing he could do. Eventually he died, but his spirit was so driven by the desire of revenge that he was reborn as Tesso,a huge rat with iron claws. Together with his summoned army of rodents, he killed the opponent monks and destroyed their monastery. Cursed Raigo continued his devastation until a shrine was built, to calm his spirit. He eventually turned into a guardian spirit, but the legend about his revenge for breaking a promise is still alive in Japanese culture.

A totally different image of the rat emerges in the western culture and folklore. Instead of bringing luck, it brings destruction and sickness. Rather than being a symbol of wealth, it represents poverty and filth. Roots to the western approach for rats can reach many aspects of life, including religion, as previously mentioned. In Islam, they are among five animals which should be killed at a sign, as they are considered dangerous. Judaism presents them as dirty crawling creatures. In Christianity, particularly rats are mentioned in the Old Testament as bringers of disease, impure and filthy creations. This label has stuck to them for centuries. During the Bubonic Plague and Witch Hunts, rats' association with the devil and demonic forces became very vivid. People used to connect them with occultism and dark magic.

But even before Christianity came to Western countries, the indiginious people from these regions have already had a rather negative perception of these rodents. Many superstitions were created in pagan folklore concerning them. Celts believed that rat-chewed items attract misfortune, and seeing rats leaving a house means approaching death. British sailors treated them as a bad omen, announcing the sinking of a ship. In Ireland many rodents accommodated in one place meant the oncoming of a war. Such events contributed to the emergence of the conviction that rats have an ominous power of foreseeing death and destruction. Ancient Romans and Greeks also perceived them as foretellers of a disaster. New myths and beliefs have been created over the years, and some are still present nowadays in many cultures.

Next to religion, history also had an enormous impact on these critters' reputation. The ubiquity and gluttony of rats, leading to crop and food supplies destruction, became a serious problem for people to deal with for many generations. The condition of towns, villages and cities was depicted in many legends and myths famous in the western countries. People started to derive inspiration from reality, in order to create scary stories or fables with morals, using the image of these animals.

Almost every child in Europe is familiar with the tale about The Pied Piper of Hamelin, German folk story from the Middle Ages, about Saxon city infested with rats. Being in desperate need of solution, it was saved by a certain rat catcher, armed only with a flute. He was able to control the animals with his music, and led them all to the lake to drown. But after the mayor refused to pay him, the piper prepared a cruel revenge. He used his flute on kids from the town and, as previously done with rats, he led them all to their deaths. Though rodents  are not a direct cause of the misery in this tale, they ignited the whole catastrophe. Rats were often presented as one big swarm, not only as being a background for gruesome events, but also sometimes as their consequences.

In Polish legend about King Popiel, mice and rats are the embodiment of justice and payment for terrible deeds. The title ruler was cruel and greedy. His people, afraid of his wrath, led a humble and quiet life. After marrying the German princess, the king decided to poison all who opposed them, along with his own son from the first marriage. After all the oppositionists died, instead of burning them, as an old Slavic custom dictates, he tossed the bodies into a lake. Though villagers were outraged by such a behavior, and afraid of Gods' anger, they were too scared to raise their voice. But shorty after the murders, they witnessed some gruesome event. A large group of rodents (in some versions mice, in some rats) emerged from the lake, and ran towards the castle. They killed every guard on their way, focused on reaching the king and queen. Popiel escaped with his family, and hid in tall, brick tower, located on the island in the middle of the lake. Unfortunately, to his dismay, creatures jumped into the water, and reached the hideout, which they easily managed to climb. Due to the legend, terrible screams could be heard in the whole town, and after the silence finally came, villagers discovered only bones left in the tower. The royal family was eaten alive.

Another famous story about supernatural rats has its roots in Great Britain. During the Victorian era, London, swarming with these rodents, became the lair of the legendary Rat Queen – a shapeshifting entity. Due to the folk tales, she was a demonic rat, able to turn into an attractive woman, who lived in the sewers beneath the capital city of England. Scavengers, called toshers, used to visit the underground, looking for coins and jewelry lost in the streets of London, often landing in the gutter. They told the stories of a young woman seducing them, and leading into the dark corner in order to use them for her own satisfaction. If she was pleased, the man was blessed with the luck of finding more valuables. But the capricious Queen could also bring doom upon a poor mortal, sentencing him to death by drowning or being eaten alive by her companion rats.

In The United States of America and Canada rats are mainly associated with Halloween, the time of celebrating death and fear. Their effigies decorate backyards and malls, together with skeletons, witches, and

zombies. They became the symbol of dread also thanks to many popular horror stories, books, and films.

Not many animals have such negative connotations as rats. Maybe only spiders or snakes can compete with them for the title of the most feared and hated creature. Yet, in the twenty-first century, more and more people start to see something more than fear, disgust, and destruction in them. We start to show more interest and fascination, rather than detestation. Though, there is still a long way for rats to go, in order to gain our trust and respect after years of being our number one enemy, there is a great chance for them to finally reach redemption.

TABLE OF CONTENTS

TABLE OF CONTENTS

I would like to thank all of the people, who helped me with this book, by providing knowledge, sharing their stories, and inspiring me. My sincere thanks to 'Lab Rescue - Adoption of Laboratory Animals' Charity, all rat owners, who allowed me to use the pictures of their precious pets (check out Rats Gone Nuts on Instagram!), my partner, Grzegorz, for always believing in me, and my mom and dad, for not throwing me out of the house the day I brought Jeffrey home.

Printed in Great Britain
by Amazon

36543684R00076